THE COIN

A Journey to Discover What It Means to Lead

JUSTIN MEARS

First paperback edition October 2019

Book design by Phillip Gessert
Edited by Claudia Volkman

ISBN 978-1-7333804-0-9 (paperback)
ISBN 978-1-7333804-1-6 (ebook)

Published by LeadOff Publishing
www.leadofllc.com

TABLE OF
CONTENTS

FOREWORD

I T's BEEN SAID that the "coin of the realm" of leadership is communication. The more neuroscience teaches us about the human brain, the more it becomes clear that mental models—simplified internal symbols or representations of the complex world around us—shape the way we take in the world. Effective leaders communicate in ways that give uncertain, complex, and ambiguous situations meaning. Metaphors matter. Narrative matters. Having a hip-pocket of useful mental models for the people and teams we lead, told through vignettes, parables, and analogies, provides an advantage of incalculable value. I've yet to meet a leader who was too clear and concise in their communication style in my nearly forty-year professional career, the last twenty-five of which has been spent developing leaders.

In that twenty-five years, I've also concluded that leader development is in large part self-determined. That is to say, one can take dozens of courses in leadership and enroll in experiential opportunities to reinforce that learning. But this won't necessarily make you a better leader. You must have a mindset, a will to be a better decision maker, a more effective communicator, a better person. For this reason, inspiration is at least as important as information.

The Coin is a book dedicated to inspiring leaders as much as it will inform them. Each chapter contains the key elements of inspiration and information designed to bring out the best in people. My suggestion is to give it a quick read, mark up the pages, write notes in the margins, and circle those lessons that have application to your personal realities. Then set the book aside but within view. When challenges arise in your personal and professional life, pull out the book, find the applicable chapter, and add to your own story. The author has set up the timeless, universal issues associated with leadership—the art and science of inspiring, informing, and directing the efforts of others toward a common purpose.

In my own leadership journey, I've found inspiration/information references extremely helpful. On my shelf are Patrick Lencioni's *The Five Dysfunctions of a Team*, William Bennett's *The Book of Virtues*, and Stephen Covey's *The 7 Habits of Highly Effective People*. They sit among hundreds, perhaps thousands, of books on my office shelves. But there's something about their accessible style and practical nature that causes me to use them more often than others. *The Coin* is drawn from the same genre. Accessibility and practicality are the purpose. That is not to say, however, that this book is simple. It raises extremely difficult matters that demand deep reflection. You must add the determined will to apply its lessons.

Justin Mears has provided everything needed by the new leader or seasoned practitioner. The reader need only to approach *The Coin* in the way it is intended to be approached. Bring your challenge, a problem-solving mindset, and an openness to applying the lessons of the book. It's all here. Make the stories your own.

Joseph J. Thomas, PhD
Director, VADM James B. Stockdale
Center for Ethical Leadership
United States Naval Academy

INTRODUCTION

ALL ACROSS THIS country and the world, there are men and women struggling to piece together what it means to be a leader rooted in character and striving for integrity. What they see from the actions of their own leaders doesn't always match what they know to be true. They are hungry for someone to actually lead them, to have their best interests at heart, to understand what it means to serve, and to spend themselves in a worthy cause.

The Coin isn't just a story about leadership. Beyond the narrative, beyond the stories, and beyond the journey of a young man trying to understand the depths of what it means to actually lead, it is a calling to all of us to make each other better; to bring each other up to our best selves. I hope that the journey traveled is one that rings true for everyone in some way.

Not every story explored in this book is going to be the most relevant for you. We all come from different backgrounds, have different experiences, and relate to different individuals in different ways. What I hope this book does, though, is serve as a calling for the need to examine the lives of those who have demonstrated the proper formation of specific character strengths and to figure out what actions would solidify those habits in our own lives. I hope that you take note of the lessons presented and then continue to search out the stories of the individuals who can best serve as the "moral exemplars" in your own life.

But most of all, I hope that you finish the book compelled to join us in our mission of being Leaders Developing Leaders. My dream is that we could start a movement, a push for real-life groups that meet, have difficult discussions, hold each other accountable, and challenge each other to achieve our own level of *eudaimonia*.

Everyone deserves a leader that wants to help them earn their own coin, to achieve a life of *arete*, to be engraved with the qualities necessary for sustained excellence in life.

The work never stops. The journey is never finished.

Leadership is exhausting. Embrace it!

CHAPTER 1

συνάντηση
THE ENCOUNTER

"A life isn't significant except for its impact on other lives."

—JACKIE ROBINSON

JOEY WALKED OUT of the boardroom, the door from the lavish twenty-fifth-floor corner office closing behind him. He needed time to process what he had just been told, what the news meant for him and his seemingly bright future at the regional manufacturer where he found himself employed.

This was his opportunity to leave his mark, to prove his worth, to be tasked with accomplishing something that would significantly impact the trajectory of the organization and his career moving forward.

He walked to the elevator and stood there, forgetting to press the button to return two floors below to his less elegant space in the high-rise building nestled in the downtown Atlanta business district.

Eventually, Greg, the company's chief operating officer, approached, pressing the button Joey had forgotten and asking the young leader if he was alright.

Snapping back to reality, Joey assured the COO that he was fine as he joined him for the ride down, still trying to wrap his head around the chance he had been given.

"I just heard the news. Congrats! That's a big-time opportunity!" the COO said, breaking the silence. "There are a lot of people around here rooting for you and your team. We know you have what it takes to lead this group. We wouldn't have chosen you for the job if we didn't. Just make sure you remember that in the coming weeks when things get tough!"

Joey politely thanked the man, attempting to make light of the moment but knowing deep down that the senior executive was right. This was his chance to show the company that he was ready for a high-level leadership position at such a young age.

Finally, the hours spent in his tiny cubicle were going to be worth it.

He let the twenty-third floor pass by, deciding that he needed to get some fresh air, hoping that would help him fully comprehend the opportunity he had just received and come up with a plan of attack when he addressed his team for the first time later that day. They would all be notified of their new assignments in short order and would be waiting for him to fill them in on the details before long.

He would be leading a group of twelve highly capable employees from a cross section of the company's departments. This task force of high performers would bring together a group with diverse skill sets and corporate knowledge, all working as a team for the first time to try and tackle one of the most pressing issues facing their organization.

Joey walked outside into the bright morning sunlight. He headed down Baker Street, his entire adult life flashing before his eyes through the glare of the cars passing by.

Only seven years had passed since he had graduated at the top of one of the country's most prestigious business schools. He quickly found himself rapidly climbing the corporate ladder, recognized for his skill and competency, and on the cusp of a twenty-fifth-floor office himself.

But this was the first time he had been asked to lead a team like this. With so much riding on the ability to create a solution to the current predicament that had put not only the company's profits but potentially its reputation at risk, Joey wasn't sure he was prepared to take on that level of responsibility.

I've been in leadership positions before, he reminded himself. As a charismatic teenager, he had been elected class president in high school. He also was a top student in the classroom and a three-sport standout on the athletic field. He had been recruited by a number of premier universities, ultimately choosing a school that would provide him the opportunity to play Division One basketball while receiving the best business education possible.

He was chosen as a team captain his senior season on the hardwood, but the role did not involve much more for Joey than leading stretching during warmups, making sure his teammates showed up to workouts, and occasionally giving a rousing half-time speech. He hadn't been empowered by the coaching staff to do more, and he was willing to let them operate as they saw necessary without any interference.

He had never really put much thought into his "leadership style," beyond deciding early on that he would try and live up to the coach's expectations and set the example for everyone else to follow. To him, that seemed to be sufficient at the time. He had been told his whole life that sports build leadership qualities, and between the hours spent on the basketball court and his business classes, he assumed he would have all the tools he needed to lead at his disposal.

Before Joey knew it, he had walked three blocks to Centennial Olympic Park, lost in his thoughts as he struggled to recall what he had learned from those leadership opportunities and classes in the past. Nothing really stood out, other than the feeling that his peers and teammates must have seen something in him to have elected him class president and team captain.

"It's not really that hard, is it?" he murmured. "Lead by example, I guess. Make sure you have your teammates' backs. Give max effort. If you do that, people will follow you."

"Sounds like some pretty good one-liners!" a voice in front of him commented.

Joey glanced up from the trail and noticed an older gentleman sitting on a bench off to the side of the path, dressed in a tattered sport coat and jeans, with a pair of loafers on his feet.

Unaware that he had spoken his thoughts out loud, Joey stared at the man, unsure how to respond.

"Can I help you?" he finally said.

"I was just pointing out that you were rattling off some pretty good catch phrases," the man said with a smile. "Lead by example. Have each other's backs. Give max effort. You know, the kind of stuff tailor-made for posters with icebergs and eagles."

Wondering if the man might be a little off his rocker, Joey politely apologized for disturbing him and looked down again, focusing in on the concrete in front of him as he attempted to get his mind back on track for his upcoming team introduction.

"You practicing for a big speech or something?" he heard the older man say as he began walking past him.

Joey was indeed hoping to give a pep talk when he was introduced to his team, but he hadn't even begun to think about what that would entail.

Not wanting to be rude but hoping he could drop the stranger a hint that he wasn't looking to be interrupted, he turned around and sarcastically answered the question.

"No sir, just brainstorming a slogan for a poster with a wolf and his pack."

"The strength of the pack is the wolf and the strength of the wolf the pack? Perhaps you would be better suited with a duck swimming in a pond," responded the old man. "You know, stay calm on top of the water, but paddle like crazy underneath!"

Joey acknowledged the running joke with a smirk and was about to walk on again when the man introduced himself.

"My name is Marcus," he said.

"Joey Cook."

"Pleasure to meet you, Joey. What brings you out for a walk in the park today?"

It was evident to Joey that he wasn't getting away without a few minutes of small talk, and he wasn't really ready to head back to work just yet, so he obliged. "I work over there," the young leader said, turning and pointing out the massive building in the skyline a few blocks away. "I needed to get out of the office and clear my head a little bit...you know, gather my thoughts."

"Well, you've come to the right place," Marcus said. "Nothing beats a stroll in the park when you have a lot on your mind. What's got you in need of a thought-gathering expedition?"

"The board of directors just gave me a major assignment. I've been entrusted with a twelve-person team made up of some of our best and brightest minds, and we've been tasked with coming up with a solution for a major issue the company is facing right now."

"That's terrific. Nothing like a big-time challenge to really bring out the best in everyone! If you don't mind me asking, what's the cause for concern?"

"Well, for me it's the ability to effectively lead this team toward some semblance of a solution. For the board, it's a matter of ensuring the proper service life of one of our major products while keeping the cost to manufacture that product as low as possible."

"Seems simple enough," declared Marcus. "Keep quality high and costs low. Sounds like a recipe for success."

"It's not that simple. We produce parts used primarily in military aircraft. Our company has been slowly moving to a more automated process, using autonomous machinery to perform the welding on specific components as a way to decrease production time and cost.

"The problem is that the machinery we are using has not been retooled for the latest operating system required to support welding on some of the higher-end raw material needed for the aircraft parts. If we use the machinery to perform the welds on the higher-end raw material, tests have shown that we will get incomplete penetration.

"If we decide to switch to a material more compatible with our current machinery, we will get sufficient welds, but the parts will be susceptible to premature failure due to fatigue caused by the lower-quality material.

"If we upgrade the machinery as well as the operating system, it will take us much longer to break even on our investments and cost significant time and money. We would have to stop production on those parts all together for weeks in order to complete the upgrade and get the operation back online. There is no way we will be able to meet our quarterly output required by our contract if that happens.

"My team has the unenviable task of coming up with a solution that keeps our operation running, maximizes profits, and increases production rate, all while ensuring that we don't sacrifice the quality of the components we produce. Just saying it out loud makes me nauseous."

"Well, please don't lose your lunch on my loafers," exclaimed the old man. "I just had Tom two benches down give them a fresh shine."

"Thanks for the sympathy," Joey muttered. "Serves me right for rambling on about my problems to a complete stranger."

"Don't be so sure. Perhaps I can help. I served in the Navy back in the day, so I understand the importance of ensuring that our aircraft have reliable parts that meet the necessary service life expected by our military members."

Joey, not wanting to downplay the man's service but unsure how that really solved his problem, replied, "That's great and all, but that isn't going to help me increase profits and the rate of production. And I haven't even mentioned the different personalities I have to satisfy along the way to make this happen."

"Hmm . . .that's a fair statement, I suppose. Perhaps I can offer you something with the potential to solve all of your challenges, from leading your team to discovering a plan of attack on the production of your high-end parts. Is that something you might be interested in?"

Joey rolled his eyes slowly, ensuring the exaggeration of the movement was noticed by his newfound companion. "Sounds perfect. If you have a lamp I could rub that would grant me three wishes, I'm sure we could come up with a solution."

Marcus chuckled. "Everyone always thinks it's a genie. I don't get it. The whole thing seems overplayed. Three wishes and then you're done? That's not going to give you the results you're looking for. You need something more...permanent."

It's official. This guy is crazy, Joey thought. *Perhaps I should check the local mental institutions to see if they are missing a patient instead of wasting any more time listening to this.*

At any rate, it was time for him get back to work. His team would be expecting that introduction before long, and they didn't have any time to waste before starting to look for an answer.

Every day without a solution meant less revenue, lower production, and for the time being, lower quality. His reputation and the reputation of the business was much too important to waste precious minutes talking to a guy who had apparently had more than one person mistake him for a genie with a magic lamp.

As he contemplated a way to politely escape, he noticed that Marcus had pulled something out from under the bench and was opening what looked like an old, worn-out briefcase.

Oh great, here we go, Joey thought to himself.

"You got some magic beans in there, too?" he asked the old man.

"Good guess, but not quite," Marcus said with a smile. "This is my coin collection. These coins have helped many a man or woman in similar situations overcome the challenges they were facing."

Joey looked down as the old man spun the briefcase around. He saw what seemed like a few dozen coins in there. They looked ancient, yet they appeared as if they had never been touched; they were as shiny as the day they were made.

Joey could see what looked like Roman numerals and inscriptions on each coin, but they were clearly all different, unique, distinct.

He had never seen coins like these, even in museums. Whatever rare currency this was, and as intrigued as he was to pick one up and inspect it, it wasn't going to make the slightest dent in helping him with his current predicament, so he avoided taking the bait.

"Unless those coins are worth around 5 million dollars each, I don't think they're going to solve my problem."

"I promise you, these coins are priceless. You won't find a collection like this anywhere."

"It looks like a rare assortment; I'll give you that. But even if that were true, I don't see how that does anything to help me out. How can a bunch of old, shiny coins make me a better leader before I go back to work this afternoon?"

Finally making a move at finalizing the conversation, Joey informed Marcus that he needed to start his trek back to the waiting task force who would be assembling on the twenty-third floor.

Marcus didn't blink or change his demeanor in the slightest. He simply turned the briefcase back around, closed it, and put it back under the bench.

"Well, good luck!" he exclaimed. "I hope you find what you're looking for. If you ever need anything, you know where to locate me. It would be my pleasure to serve you in any way I can."

Joey expected Marcus to continue talking—to try and persuade him that he needed whatever he was selling. He looked down as he started back up the path to his office, but he heard nothing.

The young leader had gone from being preoccupied about the opportunity in front of him and how he would handle leading his new team to pondering what the old man said as he left.

What I'm looking for? I don't think I was looking for anything. I just wanted a walk in the park to collect myself. What makes him think I'm looking for something? Joey's thoughts swirled. *And what did he mean by serving me in any way he can? I literally just met the man ten minutes ago.*

Joey turned around for one last glance at Marcus before walking out of the park, but there was no one on the bench previously occupied by the old man.

"Maybe Tom the shoeshine guy needed to see his coin collection too," Joey said to himself, marveling at how quickly Marcus had disappeared. He attempted to put the seemingly pointless encounter behind him and get back to what was most important: readying himself for the challenges that lie ahead.

He had no time to catch his breath upon returning to the office. Everyone was assembled in the conference room, ready to hear firsthand why they had been brought together and what was so urgent that they had been pulled away from their normal work to be incorporated in this makeshift team.

Knowing he would only get one shot at a first impression, Joey had rehearsed his lines repeatedly as he walked the three blocks back to the office.

"Ladies and gentlemen, thank you all for taking the time to join me this afternoon," he stated matter-of-factly. He glanced up just long enough to get a good look at his new teammates.

Perhaps I should have taken the time to at least look at their names or positions before kicking this off, he thought. No matter, it was too late at this point, and they would have weeks of working together to become acquainted with one another.

Several of the team members seemed to glare at him, as if to tell him they had no choice but to be there, so he should cut out the formalities and get straight to the point.

He took their glances to heart, diving right into the problem at hand.

"As many of you know, we have spent the last six months increasing automation in our military division by installing devices capable of providing welds at critical component locations. Eighty-five percent of our welding in this division has become autonomous, and with that, we have the capacity to increase our production rate as well as the profit for the company, with some projections as high as a forty-five percent increase in throughput over the next two quarters. Unfortunately, testing shows that we have a major issue on our hands."

As he explained the details of the problem, the reaction of his team was drastically different than what he had experienced when relaying the situation to Marcus.

No one appeared to see this as an opportunity; there was only concern and discord over who was to blame for the problem in the first place.

"I tried to tell them," came a voice from across the table.

Sam, one of the longest-tenured employees on the production floor and one of the most respected managers in the company, was nonchalant in confirming what he perceived as an inevitability.

"I tried to tell them that this would be the cost of going autonomous. We would lose important jobs, and then what would happen when the systems failed to provide us with the quality we were looking for? Sure, they can speed up time of production, but they can't beat the quality and care we put into each workday."

Joey hadn't considered the impact on the morale of team members who had seen friends lose jobs on the production floor. *They are probably wondering if they will be next,* he thought. But before he could try to smooth things over, he was interrupted.

"You had to know this was coming," said Cathy, one of the bright young engineers working in Research and Development. "It's a sign of the times. Everyone is moving toward more automation, and we have to adapt to the environment we are in or we risk getting left behind."

Joey tended to agree with her sentiment, but it did not sit well with the team members from the production floor.

"Well, what do I stand to gain from helping the team solve this problem?" someone shouted. "In the end, if I'm just delaying the inevitable, what's the point?"

Thinking this was his opportunity to reassure his team and

set the bar for what was expected moving forward, Joey quickly responded.

"We all have a job to do. Right now, if we don't solve this problem, the reputation of the company is at risk. We have spent too much time and effort establishing ourselves as an organization that delivers the highest quality products on time to our service members not to come up with a solution."

That sounded good, Joey thought. *Surely it would resonate with them.*

Sam chimed in again. "Everyone knows what *you* stand to gain from solving this problem. We figure out how to help the bottom line and increase profits, the board is happy, the investors are happy, and you are the knight in shining armor that saved the day."

Joey could feel his face flush, both out of embarrassment and frustration with the way this meeting was going. He knew there would be hurdles to overcome with pulling together team members from across the company's departments, but he expected they at least would collectively understand why this mattered.

Sensing the downward spiral occurring, he moved to conclude the meeting, preparing his team for the real work that would begin tomorrow. He told them they would reconvene first thing in the morning to establish working groups to brainstorm a way forward and solve the issue. Until then, he urged them to think hard about the importance of this team and what an inability to find a solution would mean.

Joey headed back to his office, sinking into his chair with the burden of responsibility weighing heavily on him. He wasn't naïve enough to think that there wouldn't be challenges in leading this team, but he didn't even know where to begin.

How would they ever start to make any headway on a solution if they couldn't even agree on the importance of the problem in the first place?

He looked over the list of employees he had been assigned.

There was Jill from accounting. He had worked with her on

several occasions and knew how talented she was with numbers. If anyone would be able to translate lost production into lost revenue, it would be her.

There were Mark and Cathy from R&D. They would be integral in creating a culture of innovation that looked beyond the obvious for a creative solution.

Then, of course, there was Sam from production. Joey sensed he would be one of the hardest to bring on board. He carried a significant level of influence, and he was clearly critical of the changes that were occurring. It didn't help that there was another member of the production department: Steve, a longtime floor team leader who would surely back Sam in all regards.

Next were Ron and Liz from manufacturing. Joey knew they had the ear of Bill, the company's VP of manufacturing who had been the catalyst behind the shift to autonomous production. Would they be committed to finding the best solution for the company—or would they simply be looking out for the manufacturing department's best interests?

John and Debbie from quality assurance were critical team members too. The quality assurance department would not settle for anything less than what the company guaranteed to deliver, and Joey knew there were already contentious feelings between QA and manufacturing.

Jenny from purchasing would be working directly with the government contracting officer to alleviate any concerns over the ability to fulfill the company's contract. She would be under enormous pressure if a solution wasn't discovered in time to meet their quarterly production goals.

Finally, there was Nick from safety. That department wasn't always given its due, but Joey knew it was critical to the success of the company. Any lost time because of injury or equipment failure would only heighten the tension between the production floor and everyone else.

There they are, my "dynamic dozen," he thought to himself, smiling at how quickly he came up with their new nickname.

But the more Joey considered the task of bringing them all together toward a solution, the more insecure he became over his ability to do so. As he gathered his belongings to head home for the evening, he thought back to the peculiar stranger he had met earlier that day.

Marcus had been so confident that he had something to offer him. Joey *was* intrigued by the coins, although he was more curious about what they actually were than how they could possibly help him bring his team together.

Regardless, he had to agree with the old man that his one-liners weren't going to be enough.

Perhaps there was more to this whole leadership thing than he thought.

CHAPTER 2

εὐδαιμονία

PURPOSE

"If we lose sight of people, we lose sight of the very purpose of leadership."

—Tony Dungy

T HE NEXT MORNING, as he prepared for the first official day of leading his new team, Joey was still at a loss for how to proceed. He had had a very restless night's sleep, tossing and turning, the discussion from the first meeting replaying continuously in his mind.

What could he have said differently to show the team the importance of their mission?

How could he convince them that, regardless of who was to blame for the problem at hand, it was going to take a collective effort to emerge victorious?

He got up earlier than normal and headed into work.

When he arrived at the corporate office, there wasn't a soul to be found on the twenty-third floor. As he sat at his desk trying to develop a plan to unify their effort toward the common goal at hand, he decided to change into his workout gear and go for a run.

The young leader made his way into the early morning light and jogged toward the park, the bustling Atlanta business district in front of him. He focused on the sound of his feet hitting the pavement and tried to block everything else out.

He hadn't even begun to break a sweat when he heard a familiar voice booming over the passing cars.

"If it isn't the slogan generator!" Marcus declared.

Joey slowed his pace, stopping in front of the local coffee shop where his new companion was sipping his morning joe.

"Good morning," he said.

"What brings you out of the glass palace this early?" Marcus replied.

"Just getting a little run in before the workday, preparing myself for day two of leading my crew."

"Well, how did the pep talk go?"

Still reeling from how ineffective the meeting had been, and not even considering what appeared to be a serendipitous coincidence that he would run into the same old man twice in as many days, Joey proceeded to fill Marcus in on everything that had transpired.

"I just don't get it. How can they not understand the importance of solving this problem? And what makes Sam think he can judge me so quickly, deciding within five minutes that I'm looking to be the company's knight in shining armor?"

Marcus listened intently. He could hear the visible frustration in the young leader's voice. Once Joey had finished, the old man paused to make certain that he was done venting and then softly asked him one simple question.

"Joey, what's your purpose?"

Joey sat down in the chair next to Marcus, looking bewildered.

"My purpose? As in what is my reason for sharing this with you?"

"No. What is your purpose?"

"What is your why?"

"Why do you come to work each day?"

"Why do you want to lead this team?"

"Why this job?"

"Why?"

Joey, taken aback, struggled to make a coherent response.

"I, um, well...to be honest, that's not a question I've ever really considered. I'm not sure I have a purpose per se. I just come to work, give it my all, and hope that's enough to earn the respect of everyone around me."

Marcus nodded as if he was anticipating Joey's answer and was ready with a follow-up question. "OK, I'll come back to that. Answer me this then, what is your company's purpose?"

Joey, a little more prepared for this one, responded, "I don't know it word for word, but we have a corporate purpose out there somewhere that talks about 'delivering what is needed to those who need it when they need it.'"

"And how does your new team fit into that purpose?"

"Well, our company doesn't really talk much about the corporate purpose. It's more just something that's on our letterhead and at the bottom of our presentations. I've always thought of it as more for our customers than us. But I suppose that without my new team, the organization can't really fulfill any part of that purpose. We won't be able to provide what is needed when it is needed to those service members who are in need of our products to carry out their own missions."

Marcus continued to nod. "And what do you envision for your team? How do you connect that purpose to the actions that will be required each day from them in order to fulfill it?"

"You've got me there," Joey responded. "That's the million-dollar question."

"Well, I don't have a million dollars, but I can share something with you that might help," the old man declared.

Joey, desperate for something that could actually benefit him and his team, decided to indulge him.

"Sure, what have you got for me?"

Marcus reached under the table and pulled out his briefcase, opening it up to reveal the same old yet shiny coins that had perplexed Joey less than twenty-four hours ago.

Now, sitting much closer to Marcus then he had been yesterday, Joey could make out the appearance of each one. They were arranged in rows, custom-fit into what appeared to be specifically ordered slots. Each one was inscribed with the same three letters: **LDL**.

Underneath each slot in the briefcase, there was a single word, etched in a foreign language that Joey didn't recognize. Marcus, sensing Joey's intrigue, picked up one of the coins and passed it to him.

"Here, take a look at the front of this one," he said.

Joey looked down at the slot where Marcus had pulled the coin.

He turned the coin over to reveal an engraved marking. It looked like a flag, old and tattered, that had been ripped in two and then sewn back together. εὐδαιμονία was inscribed below it.

"Incredible detail!" Joey exclaimed.

"That's not even the best part," said Marcus.

Joey looked at it, wondering what else could be better than the intricacies he saw.

"Flip it!"

"Flip it? Does that add to the shiny effect or something?" Joey quipped.

Marcus just laughed. "Yeah, something like that."

The young leader rested the coin on top of his thumb and gave it a toss, looking up directly into the bright Atlanta sun as he focused on catching it on its way back down.

As Joey reached out his hand to grab the coin out of midair, the sun seemed to shine even more brightly, as if he were being blinded by the light reflecting off all the buildings around him at the same time.

He squinted and then looked up, the setting coming back into focus as he searched his hand to make sure he had actually caught the coin. Joey suddenly found himself in a very different place.

Gone were the massive buildings adorning the skyline. Gone were the streets, the cars, and the coffee shop.

Frantically, he looked around, trying to process his surroundings and figure out how he had been transported to this foreign location.

He and Marcus were in the midst of a large gathering of people assembled in a wide-open field. He saw a wooden stage with twenty to thirty people on it. A man was addressing the crowd.

"What is this?" Joey shouted.

He tried to inquire further about what had happened, but Marcus put his finger to his lips, silencing the young leader and focusing his attention straight ahead.

Joey, trying to calm himself and avoid a complete meltdown, took a deep breath and tried to hear what the speaker on stage was saying.

The man appeared to be in his late sixties or early seventies, with a full head of white hair and adorned in antique formal wear. Whoever he was, he was delivering a series of impassioned remarks.

As he looked around, Joey noticed some soldiers, dressed in uniforms reminiscent of those he had seen in school textbooks.

He and Marcus had clearly traveled back in time somehow, apparently to listen to some old man give a speech about who knows what. Joey continued to look around and observe as his new surroundings began to take shape.

They were on a small hill, if you could call it that. As he looked from the hill out across the open fields in front of him, he noticed the remnants of battle, small traces of conflict that were strewn across the land. There were busted wagons and broken fences. He noticed a dented canteen and even strips of blue and gray clothing.

He turned back to the crowd and began to comprehend the magnitude of the situation. There must have been at least ten thousand people gathered here.

Some of them were listening intently, hanging on every word that bellowed from the old man's mouth.

Some were crying, moved to tears by the words being spoken.

Still others were simply meandering throughout the field, an indication that the speech had been going on for some time.

The man, who appeared to have no notes, his remarks clearly memorized for the occasion, spoke at length about what was at stake and why they were here.

He talked about ancient Athens, the burial rituals established there for heroes lost in battle. He talked of holy ground, consecrated over three all-important days that brought them together. He spoke of the gallantry and heroism on display. He recalled in great detail the events leading up to this engagement, the days and weeks that had occurred previously setting the stage for this "momentous day."

He then elaborated on those three days, talking about General Lee and General Meade, the Rebels and their cause, the Constitution, and listing civil conflicts of nations past.

He continued for what seemed like an hour or more, speaking of the time coming when the Rebellion must cease and the longing of the masses to see the "dear old flag floating" again.[1]

As he concluded his address, he spoke directly to the citizens of Pennsylvania, and it became clear to Joey exactly where they were.

This was most certainly Gettysburg, the site of one of the most critical battles of the United States Civil War, but he still had no clue who the speaker was.

Joey leaned over to Marcus in an attempt to discern some information about the man and what he was doing there.

The old man simply pointed to the stage again, not saying a word, as the speaker concluded his talk, returned to his seat, and a band began to play a hymn.

Once the applause died down, a very tall man in a suit and bow tie stood up and approached the front of the stand. As he began to address the assembled crowd, Joey's whole body tingled as the words he had heard so many times before were uttered for the very first time.

"Four score and seven years ago our fathers brought forth on this continent, a new nation, conceived in Liberty, and dedicated to the proposition that all men are created equal.

"Now we are engaged in a great civil war, testing whether that nation, or any nation so conceived and so dedicated, can long endure. We are met on a great battlefield of that war. We have come to dedicate a portion of that field, as a final resting place for those who here gave their lives that that nation might live. It is altogether fitting and proper that we should do this.

"But, in a larger sense, we cannot dedicate—we cannot consecrate—we cannot hallow—this ground. The brave men, living and dead, who struggled here, have consecrated it, far above our poor power to add or detract.

"The world will little note, nor long remember what we say here, but it can never forget what they did here. It is for us the living, rather, to be dedicated here to the unfinished work which they who fought here have thus far so nobly advanced.

---

1. Everett, Edward. "Gettysburg Address." *http://voicesofdemocracy.umd.edu/ everett-gettysburg-address-speech-text/*. Accessed 15 January 2018.

"It is rather for us to be here dedicated to the great task remaining before us—that from these honored dead we take increased devotion to that cause for which they gave the last full measure of devotion—that we here highly resolve that these dead shall not have died in vain—that this nation, under God, shall have a new birth of freedom – and that the government of the people, by the people, for the people, shall not perish from the earth."[2]

As President Abraham Lincoln eloquently expressed his sentiments, Joey couldn't help but be overcome with emotion.

This was perhaps the most famous oration in American history, and somehow he was there, observing it as if he had been a part of that moment so long ago.

He still didn't understand how this happened or why Marcus had brought him here, but right now it didn't really matter.

As Lincoln concluded his speech, the crowd hesitated, making sure the president was actually finished before breaking out into thunderous applause. The words had clearly resonated with those who had made the journey to dedicate this sacred ground.

Marcus finally spoke, his words soft and direct.

"Flip the coin again," he told Joey.

The young leader did as he requested, giving the coin another toss-up in the air, the flash of light appearing before him, the chairs they had been sitting on suddenly appearing once again underneath them.

Joey looked out at the busy morning traffic, and then he reached down for a sip of Marcus' coffee, desperate to confirm that he was back in reality.

"Still hot!" he blurted out. "Marcus, wh-what was that?"

"Wait, you really don't know what that was? Your history teacher would be ashamed of you."

---

2. Lincoln, Abraham. "Gettysburg Address." *http://www.abrahamlincolnonline.org/lincoln/speeches/gettysburg.html.* Accessed 15 January 2018.

"No, I know we just listened to the Gettysburg Address being delivered by President Lincoln. But how did we get there?"

"*Ahh* . . . the coins have the ability to transport us to a specific moment in time to learn lessons from leaders of our past in order to help shape our present and future. Pretty cool, huh?"

"It was incredible! The raw emotion emanating from every word! The solemn understanding of what had been asked of those men coupled with the hope of what their sacrifices could ultimately mean! Hearing those transcendent words spoken from Honest Abe himself! It certainly was inspiring, but who was the first man we listened to?" Joey asked.

"That was Edward Everett. He was actually the guest speaker brought in to deliver the primary remarks that day in honor of the dedication of the Soldiers' National Cemetery at Gettysburg. Lincoln was only there to deliver a few short words."

"The poor guy talked for a couple of hours and got shown up by Lincoln in only a few minutes," Joey said, laughing.

"Yeah, he clearly felt the same way; he wrote Lincoln the following day, saying 'I should be glad if I could flatter myself that I came as near to the central idea of the occasion, in two hours, as you did in two minutes.'[3]

"So, let me ask you a question, Joey. What do you think Abraham Lincoln believed that the purpose of his presidency was?"

The young leader thought for a minute, uncertain of where the old man was leading him, before finally responding.

"To end slavery, I guess?"

Marcus smiled. "That's a great answer, but...it's wrong. Abraham Lincoln passionately believed that the purpose of his presidency—and in turn, the purpose that emerged from his own being, the reason he had been elected to the nation's highest office—was the preservation of the Union.

"Sure, Lincoln was morally opposed to the idea of slavery, as

---

3. Goodwin, Doris K. *Team of Rivals: The Political Genius of Abraham Lincoln.* New York: Simon & Schuster, 2006. Page 586.

he had made known throughout his political life, but abolition was not his purpose. Lincoln declared in a response to Horace Greeley of the *New York Tribune*, 'My paramount object in this struggle *is* to save the Union and is *not* either to save or to destroy slavery. If I could save the Union without freeing *any* slave I would do it, and if I could save it by freeing *all* the slaves I would do it.'[4] You see, even though he rejected the notion of slavery, everything he did, he did in the name of preserving the Union.

"He understood his purpose clearly, and he understood what an inability to fulfill that purpose would mean for him and the nation as a whole, including abolishing slavery. Lincoln's purpose drove everything he did.

"And Lincoln surrounded himself with people who could not stand him, spoke out against him, or were flat-out different from him in every way for the sake of realizing his purpose.

"He brought his team together, not to make himself look better or for them to agree with every decision he made, but to do what was best in the name of preservation of the Union.

"His relationship with Edwin Stanton, his Secretary of War and a man who had publicly embarrassed him years before, is the perfect example of Lincoln's ability to not only act out of his purpose but also be able to rally his administration around him in the name of that purpose.

"Stanton's private secretary, A.E. Johnson, even went as far as to say that 'No two men were ever more utterly and irreconcilably unlike...yet no two men ever did or could work better in harness...fully [recognizing] the fact that they were a necessity to each other.'

"A shared purpose and a sense of empowerment through that purpose were the force that enabled Lincoln's team to operate in the roles they were most suited to perform, regardless of their personal feelings for each other."[5]

---

4. Ibid, Page 471.
5. Ibid, Page 560.

Finally, Joey jumped in, hoping he was finally picking up on something that would enable him to help his team.

"So, are you saying that if I find a way to rally my team around our purpose, we can move past all of this 'he said, she said' nonsense?"

"I'm afraid it's more complicated than that," Marcus replied. "Purpose is only the beginning. It's where we start because purpose drives everything else. Purpose gives us meaning, and only when we are *meaning-filled* can we ever achieve that which is *meaningful*, but purpose alone wouldn't be enough for Lincoln to secure the victory. Purpose simply instilled in him a dream of monumental proportions, echoed in the words you just heard."

"That the government of the people, by the people, and for the people, shall not perish from the earth!" Joey exclaimed.

"Exactly!" Marcus responded. "Purpose, our why, allows us to dream seemingly impossible dreams. Dreams that what our forefathers envisioned four score and seven years ago, conceived in liberty, and dedicated to the proposition that all men are created equal, would become a reality. That we could become what we espoused to be, and that no matter how grim the current outlook was, that dream could be realized.

"There was a direct connection between preservation of the Union and realizing that lofty ambition, but the gap between those things was frighteningly wide."

"Yeah, we still can't seem to get there today!" Joey exclaimed.

"Precisely. So it wasn't enough to have a sense of purpose beyond measure or for that purpose to foster a dream; it took an ability to cast a vision from that purpose to the dream that enabled Lincoln to see the purpose fulfilled. The purpose never wavered, even as the dream received clarity and grew to encompass more than just restoration of the Union.

"As the dream evolved, though, the strategy for how to get there shifted. What started as a means to an end became—through the Emancipation Proclamation and echoed ultimately in the most iconic two minutes ever spoken in our nation's history—a vision for the way forward.

"All of a sudden, this great struggle, which Lincoln did not shy away from, was about more than just the conflict at hand, though there was legitimate concern whether or not the great American experiment could endure it.

"Lincoln resolved that those who gave their last measure of devotion would not die in vain, and that greater than the struggle they were engulfed in, the idea echoed through the Declaration of Independence that all men are created equal would ultimately ring true for every American.

"The words that would be memorized by children and citizens for generations to come and etched in stone at his own memorial became a beacon of hope, capturing where we had been, acknowledging the reality of where we are, and charting the course for a future of where we could go and who we as a nation could ultimately be."

Joey was truly moved. He had never even considered that the effect of Lincoln's words represented his vision for the country he was so desperately trying to restore. But Joey wasn't sure how he could put this into practice.

"This is great stuff, but how do I capture all of this with my team and our situation? It all sounds so grandiose when the future of the nation is at stake, but it seems pretty mundane when it's just figuring out how to make a profit on some aircraft parts."

"Let me see if I can break it down for you a little better," Marcus said as he took the napkin in front of him and reached for a pen inside his tattered sport coat.

"Purpose, your why, is where it all starts. I truly believe everyone has a purpose, and if you are unsure what that is, you need to be working to discover it."

As he returned the coin to its slot in the briefcase, Marcus pointed at the word Joey had seen inscribed below it.

"The Greeks used the term *eudaimonia* to describe the highest human good or flourishing. This form of 'happiness' was directly connected to a sense of meaning or purpose, the noble pursuit of what was good in life.

"This is what we should all be striving to achieve, finding our own sense of flourishing and highest good, continuously working to become the best version of ourselves. Helping others on your team discover and live out their purpose is where you come in as a leader.

"If you don't know your own purpose, you'd better start there, but as a leader that's only the first step. You then have a responsibility to help those on your team figure out their purpose as well. Once you've discovered that, you can work to align those purposes with the collective purpose of your organization."

Marcus scribbled the word *PURPOSE* on the edge of the napkin. "Alignment is critical to establishing collective purpose. If you are going to try and live out daily what is represented in your corporate purpose, you have to first demonstrate alignment between that ideal and everyone's own personal why.

That's no easy task to accomplish, mind you, but that collective purpose, when properly aligned, will be the catalyst for creating in your team those dreams that seem impossible to obtain. Purpose enables dreams, provides passion and motivation to strive for those dreams, and drives commitment to realize them no matter what. The bigger the dream, the better, if you ask me."

He scribbled the word *DREAMS* on the opposite edge of the napkin. "But dreams and purpose aren't enough. There's often an enormous gap between what you know your purpose to be and the dreams that purpose has instilled in you and your team. Think of how wide the gap must have seemed to Lincoln at the time. The gap is full of doubt and uncertainty, fear and insecurity. If you let it, the gap will cripple your team, making the obstacles seem even bigger than the dream, with no way to get around them. The way to the other side isn't around the obstacles, though, but through them, and you cross that terrifying gap with vision."

Marcus continued to scribble furiously. "Imagine vision as a bridge between purpose and your dreams."

Joey could see the drawing beginning to take form.

"You see, passion and motivation without a vision are wasted energy. Casting that vision is a leader's art. We can't all capture a vision so eloquently in two minutes like President Lincoln did, but great leaders are able to take that purpose, encourage those dreams, and then align them all through a common vision of how to get there. Vision connects every action we take from that lofty dream back to purpose. What that bridge looks like will constantly evolve; it may even change its shape or add lanes over time."

"Great, now I've got to build aircraft parts and bridges at the same time?" Joey asked sarcastically.

"Yes. Leaders are the architect of that bridge. As the architect, you are responsible for what that bridge will ultimately look like, but you have to make sure everyone on the team feels they have a part to play in the creation of it, or you won't have much buy-in when it comes time to labor during its construction.

"It reminds me of the story of JFK and the janitor. President Kennedy was on a visit to NASA in 1962 to drum up support for the Apollo missions less than a year after declaring in front of Congress his ultimate goal of putting a man on the moon within the decade. He came upon a janitor cleaning his mop in one of the closets adjacent to the hangar. Not wanting to be rude, the president spoke to the janitor and politely asked him, 'What do you do here?'

"Without skipping a beat, the man replied, 'Mr. President, I'm helping put a man on the moon.'

"That's an alignment of purpose from top to bottom. From the astronauts preparing for space travel to the custodial staff, that's communicating the importance of each individual in accomplishing the vision. Everyone must feel that their roles matter, and they must be empowered to have a say in what the vision ultimately becomes, helping to draft a blueprint that captures the why and connects it to the dream. That blueprint, which they are then encouraged to participate in imagining, becomes the goals you empower the team to create."

He scribbled some more, writing above the bridge he had drawn: GOALS ARE THE BLUEPRINT.

"A great vision without goals, without a blueprint for its construction, is just wasted time. Goals provide us with a map of what that bridge looks like, piece by little piece, down to the finest detail. They provide concrete, definitive building blocks to translate that vision into reality, to take your purpose and see it realized as it is connected to your dreams. Goals provide focus, direction for that purpose-driven energy, and resolve to see the vision to fruition."

Joey thought for a moment, trying to comprehend Marcus' analogy, before realizing there was something missing, in his opinion.

"How do I ensure that the bridge doesn't just collapse into that pit of struggle and fear you were talking about? How do I make sure it's built correctly?"

"That's a great question, son. Every bridge, every building in the world, must be built to the proper code. If it isn't constructed up to code, it will crumble. The building code isn't simply a set of rules one must follow for the sake of following the rules. The code is backed up by physics; it's a way to measure the effectiveness of the building and a means to provide every passenger that travels that bridge the certainty and assuredness of the structural integrity with which it was constructed. The standards your team operates with are that code."

He took his pen and wrote STANDARDS ARE THE CODE.

"Standards aren't just rules to follow. Standards are a part of the very fiber of your organization and team. They are norms of behavior that represent who you are and what you are about. Standards are derived from the values you have identified as most important to your team and organization, and they provide a mechanism to quantify the effectiveness of your bridge, a way to ensure the structural integrity of your team's creation, and an assurance to anyone who is a part of accomplishing the vision that things were done the right way using a method everyone can be proud of.

"Standards derived from the proper prioritization of your collective values drive the daily actions and decisions you make as you construct your vision. Just as you are the architect overseeing the blueprint, you are also the building inspector responsible for ensuring that what your team constructs is up to code.

"You must figure out what those collective values are in order to create the proper standards that reflect who you are as a team, and then you must be consistent and intentional in communicating and exemplifying what it will take to construct to the proper code. Your team needs to know what success looks like for each of them in their specific role. They need to know how their individual success impacts the team's success, and they need to know what is expected of them in order to get there.

"You see, your purpose and vision have to be much more than mere words at the bottom of a letterhead. You must live them out daily for them to really take hold.

"Your team's actions will simply be a reflection of the standards you have set. As a leader, it's up to you to set the example daily for what those standards, that 'code,' will be. And as the building inspector, you must be willing to hold everyone around you accountable to that code if you ever want to have a bridge worth crossing.

"At the end of the day, it doesn't matter what you say the standards are. The standard always becomes what you allow in your presence! As the leader, and for those that you empower to lead as well, you must ensure that the standard you walk by is the standard you are willing to accept. It's all a part of your job as the building inspector. One small component of the bridge that isn't built up to your code can have a devastating ripple effect on the entire vision.

"The standards must be nonnegotiable because all of those

daily actions over time, little by little, enable you to see the blueprint become the reality, to ultimately fulfill your purpose and accomplish your purpose-inspired dreams."

Joey looked down at his watch, almost cutting Marcus off before he could finish.

"Oh man, I totally lost track of time. This has been incredible. Thank you, thank you, thank you! I honestly don't know how I can repay you for the opportunity you just gave me to witness such an iconic moment, and for everything you have shared with me, but I really have to go. My team is probably busy at work, constructing a bridge with no idea where it begins, ends, or what it looks like."

Marcus laughed and handed Joey the napkin. "Here, take this. Use it as your guide, and always remember, you set the tone as the leader. You are responsible for the construction of your team's vision, but if you don't help everyone else tap into their purpose, they will never know how long their own bridge needs to be to realize their dreams.

"Everyone deserves a leader who seeks their highest good and knows how to help them get there. The importance of a leader willing to empower that *eudaimonic* flourishing in each and every person they are in charge of cannot be overstated."

Joey began to slowly walk away, staring at the napkin in front of him.

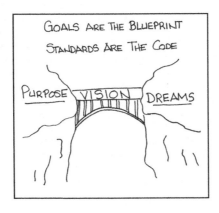

As he turned to cross the street, it occurred to him that, although he was grateful for Marcus' insight, he still had no idea what his purpose was or how he would discover it for himself.

"Hey, how will I know what the purpose is for me?" he shouted over his shoulder.

Marcus' faint voice could be heard as the young leader continued across the busy intersection.

"Who said your purpose was about you?"

CHAPTER 3

πιστεύω

BELIEF

"Leadership is communicating to people their potential so clearly that they come to see it in themselves."

—STEPHEN COVEY

A s SOON AS he got back to his office, Joey pulled the napkin out of his pocket and began to scribble down everything he could remember from his adventure.

He was still in shock, unconvinced of the reality of what he had experienced, but eager to put into practice everything he had learned from Marcus.

Over the next several weeks, he worked hard to establish a sense of collective purpose among his team.

He still wasn't certain what his own personal purpose was, and he wasn't sure what the old man's last words to him meant, but he had poured himself into discovering how his team members defined their why.

When they met as a team the first day, Joey explained the bridge to them, setting their efforts toward an understanding of the corporate purpose and how, when aligned, their own individual purposes could collectively inspire implausible dreams. He described the role of a bold vision in connecting purpose to those dreams, and he shared how they would need specific goals and standards of operation in order to achieve any of this.

He told them he understood that the vision was his responsibility, but he wanted them all to have a role in its creation. He shared honestly that he didn't have a clue as to how they were going to realize their purpose, but he echoed his belief that there was a need for their product and everything they did needed to be focused on delivering to meet that need.

After that meeting, Joey thought back to the times he had been in leadership positions before. He wondered what a sense of purpose, a rock-solid vision, intentional goals, and nonnegotiable standards would have done for those teams. Perhaps they would have won a few more basketball games.

Joey spent the next several days meeting with each member of his team, asking them what they felt their why was and how they saw it playing into the company's overall purpose. He wasn't surprised to hear from several team members that this was the first time anyone in the company had ever asked them these questions, since until a few days ago, it was a foreign concept to him as well.

For some on the team, it seemed almost liberating to put into words what they felt deep down was their true meaning.

Mark said he felt he was there to find creative solutions to make things better and easier for others. Finding innovative ways to improve gave him fulfillment.

For Debbie, it was all about providing a better life for her family than what she had as a child growing up impoverished in the inner city.

Nick had witnessed a gruesome injury to an employee nearly ten years ago, and he moved into the Safety Department because he felt called to help prevent any other families from going through the accident he had seen.

Ron had served in the military, enlisting in the Army out of high school and serving overseas in Iraq and Afghanistan, and he felt a calling to continue to provide the best capabilities possible to the country's service members whose lives were on the line.

As Joey sat with each team member, he began to realize that in order to help them fulfill any individual purpose, achieve any personal dreams, or create a vision for themselves, he needed to know more about them, their lives, where they came from, and what they wanted for their futures.

The relationships he began to develop as a result of this seemed immediately deeper and more genuine than any he had previously created on a quid pro quo basis to this point in his career.

It felt real, and a sense of satisfaction welled up inside of him whenever he encouraged someone on his team to open up and talk about themselves. Suddenly, it was about more than just work to him, but he also knew that if they didn't produce results, none of this would matter.

As he strived to focus each and every team member toward a realization of how their individual purposes aligned with the corporate purpose, Joey sensed a growing collective understanding of why all of this was necessary.

Not everyone had bought in, however.

Sam was still very vocal in his assertion that this was an inevitable outcome with no real solution. Cathy seemed equally convinced of the future of automation regardless of this current setback, and Liz seemed unsure of Joey and the sudden shift in his approach.

Nonetheless, the team began to put its collective brainpower to work with a mostly unified understanding of the importance of their undertaking. They seemed to be making a conscious effort to find a solution, regardless of how invested they were personally in the company's vision.

And yet nothing seemed to change.

No one had been able to pinpoint a good answer that didn't involve lower quality, higher cost, or a complete halt to production.

The company had been forced to bring in a slew of temporary workers, much to Sam's chagrin, eliminating the automation at the critical fault points. This had slowed the production rate significantly, cost more in labor, and with the autonomous machinery sidelined, cost significantly more to get the parts out the door. Everyone was feeling the pressure.

Joey, even with his sense of satisfaction about the relationships he was building, had been unable to take that collective purpose and find one of those big dreams Marcus mentioned. He couldn't find any semblance of a vision for how to get there either, and without that, he had a hard time nailing down specific goals to serve as his blueprint or establish the necessary standards to achieve what they wanted.

He felt he was failing as their leader, and as his confidence wavered, he was overwhelmed with doubt and uncertainty, the gap widening just as Marcus had warned him about. Feeling stuck in a daily spiral of unproductiveness, he decided it was time to seek out his new mentor for advice. Perhaps the old man had another coin in his collection that could provide him with more answers.

He set out down the same path he had previously traveled, past the coffee shop down to Centennial Olympic Park, past the bench where Marcus had been that very first time, but after covering each and every square inch of the park, there was no sign of the old man anywhere.

Marcus had told Joey he would be there when Joey needed him, and he certainly felt like he needed Marcus now.

This is crazy, he thought. *Why did I ever think I could just walk out the door and the old man would be waiting for me as if he didn't have anything better to do than sit around anticipating my every need?*

Feeling discouraged, he had no desire to head back to the office. It was Friday and he had sent the team home early for the weekend, thanking them for their efforts over the past few weeks and telling them to spend the next couple of days recharging. It was the least he could do as their leader since he felt personally responsible for their lack of progress.

He looked past the park and noticed the College Football Hall of Fame across the street.

Joey was an avid sports fan; he was especially fond of college football, and yet he had been too busy since moving to Atlanta to ever visit the Hall of Fame. He decided that spending time in a place that celebrated one of his favorite pastimes was probably better than heading home for the day, so he made his way to the entrance, paid for a ticket, and walked into the lobby.

After he entered the building, Joey looked up at the wall of helmets representing teams across each division of intercollegiate athletics.

"Man, there have definitely been some great leaders running these programs," he said out loud. "I wonder how they are able to take a new team each year and shape their vision so they reach the ultimate goal? With such high performers on every team, the competition is fierce, and only one gets to hoist the trophy in the end."

"Who is your favorite?" came a familiar voice standing next to him.

"Geez, you scared me!" Joey said, startled. "How is it you always seem to find me?"

"One of the perks of my profession," Marcus said, laughing.

"Well, you don't have to sneak up on people. A little warning would be nice," Joey replied with a smirk.

"Thanks for the feedback. I'll definitely take that into account in my daily reflection for how I can improve."

"You spend time each day thinking about your interactions with others and how to better those exchanges in that level of detail?"

"Another topic for another day, son. One step at a time. How have things been going with the team?"

"I definitely feel as though we've made some really good progress. Most of them seem to be on board with our purpose. I have kept that the focus as best I could," Joey answered.

"And what about you? Have you made any progress on discovering your own purpose?" Marcus asked.

"I haven't been able to pinpoint my exact why, but these last few weeks have certainly shown me some things about myself. I've gotten more satisfaction out of getting to know my team than I ever did squeezing out a few extra dollars for this company. And I've gotten even more enjoyment out of them opening up and sharing their own dreams with me. Beginning to feel like we are actually becoming a team reminds me of why I enjoyed sports so much growing up, and it's reinvigorated me in a way nothing else has since joining the corporate ranks. But I haven't been able to discover any of those big dreams or come up with a vision that will help us find a solution to our challenges. And without those, it's been hard to identify specific goals or standards to get us there."

"Just so we're clear, this isn't something that's going to magically change overnight," Marcus replied. "It requires consistency, and for it to become habitual, it takes time. Also, the goals don't drive the standards.

"You don't design a blueprint and then go back to make sure it is up to the proper code. You design that blueprint with an understanding of exactly what is necessary to ensure it meets the requirements already established by the code. The code, the standards—derived from those values that represent who you are—have to drive what is required in the blueprint."

"Well, even if I figure out exactly what is expected, what we value, and what the standards are, the problem still seems insurmountable at this point," Joey said. "We haven't made any progress toward a real solution, and to be honest, I'm kind of just hoping for a miracle."

"Hey, hope in the future gives you power in the present!" Marcus exclaimed.

"For someone opposed to one-liners, that was a pretty good one," the young leader shot back.

"I'm not opposed to one-liners at all. Mantras can be powerful tools if they are communicated consistently and backed up with daily actions that reinforce them. Here, let me show you where that one came from," Marcus said, pulling a coin out of his pocket and handing it to Joey.

It was exquisite, just like the Lincoln coin from a few weeks earlier, with the same numerals engraved on one side. He turned it over and saw a mountain peak, with a small flag flying on top, the word πιστεύω inscribed perfectly underneath.

"Well, are you going to look at it all day, or are you going to give it a toss?" Marcus asked.

Joey didn't hesitate. Throwing the coin in the air, the flash of light surrounded him as he caught the glittering object as it fell back to the ground.

This time Joey was prepared for the changes. He immediately looked up in anxious excitement to see where he had been transported.

He scanned the room; there was no large crowd or stage. This building was much more modern, and it seemed almost familiar.

Having spent many a night at post-game press conferences in his playing days, it was clear that this was set up for a similar event. There was a long table with microphones up front, and a gathered assembly of media anxiously awaiting a group to approach and deliver some remarks.

As he looked closer, their location became evident. Nearly everyone was wearing orange, and tiger paws adorned the room from top to bottom.

"Clemson! Really? You brought a Bulldog fan to Clemson?" he remarked snidely in Marcus' direction.

"Hey, you never answered my question about your favorite team, but I promise this will be worth your time."

As Joey tried to think of another witty comeback, the anticipated group made their way to their seats. Two men sat down behind the tiger paw-adorned microphones, wearing suits complete with tiger lapels.

An older gentleman, who introduced himself as Terry Don Phillips, athletic director at Clemson University, spoke first. He shared how excited he was about this moment as he looked to his right and introduced Dabo Swinney to those in attendance as the new permanent head coach of the Clemson Tigers. Phillips helped him put on an orange jacket to commemorate the occasion.

Coach Swinney then took the time to say some words about what this moment meant for him, a first-time head coach of a major college football program.

As Joey sat and listened, he thought intently about what was taking place. He knew this story well, having followed it closely the last few years as the Tigers clawed their way to prominence among the college football elite.

A team that had its heyday in the 1980s but vastly underperformed since then was turning to a first-time head coach who had never even served as an offensive or defensive coordinator prior to taking the job.

That was unprecedented in the sport.

Everyone always had to work their way up the ranks, proving themselves at each and every stop before anyone would dare to put them in the top position, yet Mr. Phillips felt adamant that Coach Swinney was the right man for the job after giving him a trial period as interim coach that year.

As Joey listened to Coach Swinney talk, it became evident that *he* believed *he* was the right man for the job as well, and he was confident that he could help Clemson not only regain its previous glory but also soar to new heights.

Coach Swinney talked about his secret to success. He talked

about putting your eyes on the Lord, not quitting, and believing in yourself. He spoke about dreaming big dreams, and about having a sense of belief that those dreams can come true.

He talked about humility. He thanked those who were giving him a chance and who believed in him as the right choice for the job. He concluded by saying that he believed wholeheartedly that they could achieve their goals at Clemson, that they could recruit the best student-athletes, graduate them, and win a championship.

Swinney finished his comments and began to take questions from reporters. One reporter asked, "Do you feel that Clemson is taking a gamble on you because of your lack of head coaching or even coordinator experience?"

Coach Swinney's expression was completely unchanged as he replied simply but emphatically, "No!"[1]

Joey began to murmur to himself. "I mean, any coach would probably say something similar in their introductory press conference. Hindsight is 20/20 I suppose, but who would have thought that this hire would lead the Tigers to a national championship in just eight years?"

"He did!" Marcus answered back, pointing to the head coach emotionally accepting his new role and achieving one of his personal dreams. "Belief is so much more than just words."

Marcus motioned for Joey to follow him. "I want to show you something else."

Marcus led Joey through the West Zone of the stadium and into the football facilities where the team's meeting room was located. He turned on the lights and gave Joey a chance to look around the room.

"What stands out to you?" he asked his young friend.

There were slogans galore, reminders of what was expected

---

1. TigerNet.com. "Dabo Swinney emotional as he is named Clemson head football coach." Online video clip. YouTube. 25 Nov 2014. *https://www.youtube.com/watch?v=3jqITI2XETc&t=1512s*

and what a Clemson Tiger football player should represent. There would be more to come in future years, phrases that would articulate the culture of the program as the head coach refined his vision and standards for Clemson football, but it was evident to Joey what he was supposed to notice right now.

He pointed to a sign affixed to the wall in the room that had just one word: *BELIEVE*.

Marcus took the coin from the young leader's hand and gave it another flip.

Joey, expecting to arrive back at the College Football Hall of Fame, was surprised to see that they had been transported to yet another moment in time. As he looked up, he noticed National Championship logos covering the locker room where they were now standing.

"Ah, you've brought me to where the belief came to fruition—to see the result of fulfilling the vision and realizing the dream," Joey told Marcus. "I'm here to see the Tigers celebrate their first National Championship since 1981!"

As he looked around, though, there wasn't any indication of a team emerging as the victors in their penultimate bout. Instead, there were dejected looks everywhere, tears being shed, hugs of solace being given, and a silence that was only broken as the team's emotions got the best of them.

Joey quickly realized that Marcus hadn't brought him to Tampa, Florida, the site of the 2017 National Championship where Clemson toppled mighty Alabama.

No, it was the year prior, the 2016 National Championship when the Tigers came up just short against the Crimson Tide dynasty.

Before Joey could retract his assumption, the same man he had just witnessed taking the job a few years ago entered the room and began to take account of his defeated and weary team.

Coach Swinney began by thanking his seniors for everything they had given to the program and for the bar they had set for Clemson football. He told them how proud he was of them and that he only regretted they would not get another shot at redemption.

He talked about the pain of defeat only for a minute, and then, as quickly as he addressed their failure, he turned his attention immediately to the next season.

In the midst of a crushing loss on the biggest stage, just moments after seeing their dreams slip away after a series of fourth-quarter mistakes, with the grass stains still fresh on their jerseys and the players still sweating from laying it all on the line, Swinney turned their attention to the future.

He spoke of the next year, how excited he was for what was ahead, and how the best was yet to come. He began to instill in them at that moment a sense of belief that they would be right back in this game in 365 days with a chance to cement their legacy and finish what they had started.[2]

Marcus didn't even wait for Coach Swinney to stop talking. Knowing Joey had seen all he needed to see, he flipped the coin once again, and the two of them arrived back in the busy lobby of the Hall of Fame.

"You see, Joey, hope in the future does give you power in the present. That's one of Coach Swinney's famous sayings. Hope is essential; it is critical to success. Without hope, why even start the journey? But hope by itself isn't going to get you where you want to go. You must move from hope to belief. Those two, when coupled together, have the chance to take you from occasional success to sustained excellence," Marcus explained.

"Swinney knew from the beginning what was going to be required to win a National Championship at Clemson. Before 'Bring your own guts,' before 'Doing the common things in an uncommon way,' before 'Best is the standard,' and before 'Bloom where you are planted' ever entered the lexicon of Clemson play-

---

2. Gordon, Jon. *The Power of Positive Leadership: How and Why Positive Leaders Transform Teams and Organizations and Change the World*. Hoboken: Wiley Business, 2017.

ers, Coach Swinney knew the first thing he had to do was to create an attitude of belief. Everyone else was telling them what they can't do, what's never been done, and what they hadn't done. 'You win on the inside before you ever win on the outside,' he said.[3]

"Those sayings would come to represent a Clemson football player. They would become the embodiment of Coach Swinney's vision, which was deeply connected to his purpose of building men of character, helping them be the best version of themselves in every aspect of their lives, and serving their heart as well as their talent.

"But before any of that could take hold, Swinney knew that his team needed to believe in the dream he had for them. They needed to believe what was possible at Clemson, and he needed to back that up through his and his coaching staff's daily actions.

"That's why when you walked in that meeting room there was a single word for his team to see every day: BELIEVE. Coach Swinney truly felt that before anything could change on the outside, his players had to change on the inside; they had to believe success was possible.

"And it wasn't just the 'outside' experts that didn't fully comprehend the expectations Coach Swinney had for the program. It was found at Clemson as well. Coach Swinney often told the story of how he cut off a member of the board of trustees in a meeting when he was just the interim coach after the board member said that all he wanted was for Clemson to become like the great programs, the blue chips of college football like Florida and Michigan.

"Coach Swinney said that wasn't his vision for the Tigers. His vision was that those programs would want to be like Clemson.

"That vision for his team can be found in extreme detail in

---

3. Hale, David M. "The Tao of Dabo Swinney." *ESPN*, 31 Dec 2017. *http://www.espn.com/college-football/story/_/id/21916855/clemson-tigers-dabo-swinney-culture-alabama-crimson-tide-nick-saban-process*. Accessed 10 Feb 2018.

a three-ring binder several inches thick. It contains his blueprint for success at Clemson, how to handle every single part of the program from recruiting, to strength and conditioning, to practice, to nutrition, to player development, and everything in between. And on the top of page one of that book is a single word: *Attitude*.[4]

"Coach Swinney instilled in his team an attitude of belief that said no more excuses, no more complaining about the weather, what time we play, or what uniform we are wearing. No more worrying about who, what, where, or when—we focus on *how*.[5]

"No more just *hoping* to win. Remove the negativity. Be enthusiastic. Take pride in the little things. *Expect* to win. It all comes back to belief, and belief, according to Coach Swinney, is a powerful thing."[6]

Joey cut his mentor off. "This all sounds pretty pie in the sky to me. I'm supposed to just believe that we are going to succeed and then once we believe, it's going to happen?"

"That's not the point I'm trying to make," Marcus retorted. "You said you were hoping for a miracle. I'm here to tell you that hope is essential, but hope isn't a plan. Hope says, 'I really want something to happen.' Belief requires action.

"Belief says, 'I have decided that something *will* happen, and I have confidence that even without empirical evidence that says with 100 percent certainty that it will ever occur, I have *decided* in my mind and heart that it is true.'

"Belief takes hope and raises the bar. Belief is an expectation! There is power in belief, especially when that individual belief is

---

4. Ibid

5. Positive University. "Jon Gordon and Coach Dabo Swinney Talk About Positive Leadership." Online video clip. YouTube. 14 Sep 2017. *http://positiveuniversity.com/coach-dabo-swinney/#lg=1&slide=0*

6. Hayes, Matt. "Believe: Dabo Swinney's First Word at Clemson and the Key to the Tigers' Rise." Bleacher Report, 6 Jan 2017. *http://bleacherreport.com/articles/2685518-believe-dabo-swinneys-first-word-at-clemson-and-the-key-to-the-tigers-rise*. Accessed 10 Feb 2018.

strong enough to extend to the entire team, when it becomes a collective belief that something will occur that hasn't happened yet.

"Belief is deeply connected to purpose. It emerges out of those enormous dreams when you are casting your vision for your team. It says, 'Not because of *me*, but because of *we*, there will be a way forward.' Belief comes out of the core of who you are, and it's something you can't fake. You must be genuine and authentic in your approach. Your team doesn't need you to be a Halloween leader, wearing a mask and pretending to be something you aren't or believe something you don't. They need you to actually believe and *lead* them in a way that inspires them to believe as well.

"When you have this level of belief, then it's not all 'pie in the sky,' as you said. This kind of belief, rooted in your soul and connected to your purpose, provides you with the ability to have an unquestioned awareness of your situation and honesty about where you stand.

"As counterintuitive as it might sound, belief keeps you grounded. When the gap of fear, worry, or doubt creeps in, your bridge can become covered in a haze of uncertainty that restricts your visibility. This can actually breed a lack of awareness, and you can start to see things how you wish they were rather than how they actually are because you are simply hoping the fog will clear.

"With belief you don't have to pretend that everything is going perfectly, because you trust your process, you have confidence in your purpose, your vision is solid, your standards are necessary—and to use some of my old pilot lingo, your bridge is CAVU (Ceiling And Visibility Unlimited).

"Think back to what we just experienced. In the immediate aftermath of losing the most important game of his head coaching career, that attitude of belief, habituated over time and now simply an extension of who he was, emerged from Coach Swinney as he continued to point out that the best is *always* yet to come.

"His star player, All-American quarterback Deshaun Watson,

would say after the fact that there wasn't a player in that room who didn't truly believe they would be back there next year."

Joey continued to wonder if this would actually work. "Okay, let's say I adopt this attitude of belief, and this becomes a part of who I am at my core. How do I extend that belief to my team like Coach Swinney did?"

"It's pretty simple, I think. You need to believe in them more than they believe in themselves," Marcus replied. "Belief says, 'I know what you are capable of, and I want to help you get there.'

"If we really want that *eudaimonic* flourishing for everyone, then we believe in others and what they can accomplish, and we work to convince them of that possibility in themselves, holding them accountable to the standards we know will get them there.

"Belief says, 'Even if your own bridge is surrounded in fog, even if you can't see directly in front of you, you can join up behind me. It may be uncomfortable, you may not always like the feeling of uncertainty that comes with it, but if you put your trust in me, I'll lead you until your surroundings are clear too.'

"That's why even at halftime the following year, with the Tigers behind on the scoreboard, unsure of how they were going to win, and staring at a second defeat in as many years, Swinney's belief continued to shine through. He told his team that he didn't know how they were going to win, but he knew they were going to win.

"There was no doubt in that locker room what the outcome would be. His team believed just as much as he did, and they all knew they had prepared the right way and it was only a matter of time until they had their breakthrough.

"When all was said and done, a 35-31 victory secured on an epic final drive down the field, a touchdown thrown with one second to go from an All-American quarterback to a former walk-on wide receiver, Coach Swinney would declare for everyone to hear: 'At the top of the mountain, that Clemson flag is flying.'

"And it wasn't because of some upset, regardless of what the experts declared. No, the Tigers absolutely expected the outcome they got, and it could be traced back to the belief instilled in them by their head coach."[7]

Marcus sensed that he had overloaded the young leader, who sat staring at him, wheels turning as he attempted to absorb everything that had been shared with him.

"I think that's probably enough for you to think about right now," the old man said softly. "Just know that you can't simply hope for a miracle and expect your team to magically achieve success. To be an overachiever, you need to be an overbeliever."[8]

7. TigerNet.com. Dabo Swinney postgame press conference after winning National Championship." Online video clip. YouTube. 9 Jan 2017. *https://www.youtube.com/watch?v=zkzKeLuEt6E*
8. Swinney, Dabo. Quote.

CHAPTER 4

Δέσμευση
COMMITMENT

"Individual commitment to a group effort—that is what makes a team work, a company work, a society work."

—Vince Lombardi

Joey spent the weekend pondering what Marcus had shared with him about making belief a habit. He thought back to his days as a student-athlete, in particular, his senior season of basketball.

Having seen what Coach Swinney had accomplished, that level of assuredness seemed antithetical to what had happened to Joey's team that year.

From day one, they were in rebuilding mode, and their coaches treated everything that way. It was evident from the first practice that no one really believed the team had a chance to do anything special. They were less talented than their conference opponents, and early on Joey had made up his mind that was OK.

He never believed in his teammates the way he saw the Clemson Tigers believe in each other. At the time, he attributed his lack of belief to realism, to accepting what they were given. As their captain, he focused more on ensuring that everyone was enjoying their last ride together than competing for a title.

This wasn't to say they weren't still trying their best to beat their opponents. Joey had felt that the team was giving its all, but there was no real progress throughout the season, no purpose, no big dreams, no vision, and certainly no defined standards of expectation. The more he thought about it, the more he realized his culpability in permitting that attitude of mediocrity and complacency to exist on his team.

As Joey's thoughts drifted back to his current team, he started to wrap his mind around the standards that needed to be in place for them to succeed.

It quickly dawned on him that in the same way "Best is the standard" applied to Clemson, it also applied to his group as well.

"But what does 'best' look like for us?" he asked himself. "And what values lend themselves to creating this idea of excellence in everything we do?"

Joey decided that before he could focus on the collective values that would define the team's standard of "best," he should probably consider what his own personal values were.

He had never really made an effort to categorize or prioritize his values, but as he did, he found it enlightening.

Finding the time to write down the traits he valued provided him with a sense of awareness and understanding of who he was and what was most important to him.

He started to think about whether or not he actually demonstrated the things that he held dear.

Did his work ethic shine through?

Was he actually a good son, brother, and friend?

Did he demonstrate loyalty to his team and company?

Was he honest with others even when it wasn't easy?

Was he a person worthy of trust and respect?

The more he thought about these questions, the more he began to discover that the things he valued, such as teamwork, loyalty, honesty, responsibility, and dependability, were the same values that could be construed from the individual purposes his team had shared with him the last few weeks.

Suddenly, in a moment of clarity, he realized that it was definitely obvious what "best" looked like for their team.

"Best" meant that quality could not be sacrificed for any reason. If they sacrificed quality, how could they really be providing what is needed to those that need it? Providing a lower quality product was insincere, and it went against everything his company was supposed to stand for. It certainly didn't demonstrate a standard of excellence.

Quality also meant living out the values that were important to him and his team.

Quality meant pride in a job well done.

Quality was directly related to dependability.

Quality was the right thing to do.

As the dream began to take shape, the gap below his bridge started to widen in his mind from their purpose, just as Marcus had indicated would happen. Fear and doubt began to creep in.

Deciding that lower quality of any kind was off the table surely would mean opposition from some folks in the company.

It would mean more stress and pressure on his team to find a solution.

It more than likely would mean the inability to meet quarterly goals.

The more he considered it, though, the more certain he was that this was the right way forward, and the clearer his vision for his team reaching a solution became.

He began to take stock of everyone's role in making this happen. Without a doubt, this would be a team effort, and he would need everyone on board.

It's not like I've been given a team of rejects either, he thought. *They gave me some of the best minds and best employees to work with. We have the most creative brains in the company. We have our best accountant. We have a QA team that wants nothing more than to deliver the highest quality product.*

"The pieces are all there," he began to tell himself.

Maybe he was still working on believing in himself and his team at the level he witnessed just the other day, and he knew he wasn't going to get there over the course of one weekend, but he was eager to attack the following week with a newfound enthusiasm.

On Monday Joey made his way to the twenty-third floor with a level of optimism that had been missing recently. As the team trickled in to start their workday, he was there to greet them, anxious to chart the way forward.

Over the weekend he even made his own sign, indicating to everyone exactly what he expected in the coming weeks. It wasn't quite as nice as the one Coach Swinney had designed for his players, but as everyone took their seats for the morning meeting, the word QUALITY was taped to the wall for the entire team to see.

He explained his dream to them—that regardless of their current situation, they would deliver products of the highest quality on time, and in doing so, they would fulfill their purpose.

He unfolded a vision for them of how this would happen, pointing to each and every member of the team and explaining the important role they played in the success of the team and what it would collectively take to make the vision a reality.

There would be no sacrificing quality. This ran counter to the values that were important to the company and the values his team had expressed to him over the last several weeks. He told them he believed they had the right group of people assembled to make this happen.

He concluded the meeting, expecting a round of applause from his rousing speech.

Instead, he was met with glances of uncertainty, the team clearly questioning what he had suggested.

As they slowly made their way out of the conference room and back to their desks, Sam and Liz both lagged behind to confront their young leader. Sam was the first to speak up.

"Joey, look, I appreciate your vigor and excitement, but I've been around this company for twenty years, and what you said ain't happening. The bottom line is the only thing that matters around here. If you refuse to give in, they will just find someone willing to make the bottom line work for them. You young guns are a dime a dozen. Everyone here knows this team was put together to save face. We're here to find a temporary Band-Aid, to stop the bleeding enough to avoid any major catastrophe, and I'm just here to make it to my pension in a few years."

Joey, a little bit taken aback at Sam's cynical outlook, tried to reassure him that not sacrificing quality was possible and that they needed his expertise and influence to make it happen, but it didn't seem to matter.

Liz was even more adamant that his plan was never going to work. She explained to him that automation would be the future come hell or high water, and that when the crunch started to be felt, the company would surely sacrifice quality to keep a respectable bottom line until the systems could be upgraded properly or the next wave of machinery was brought online.

As the negativity crept back in, taking away from the fresh optimism that had fueled his new outlook on the situation, Joey trudged back into his office and slumped down in his chair.

"Have I really just set us up for failure?" he asked himself. "It seems so clear to me that this is the right thing to do. Otherwise, we aren't living up to who we proclaim to be. But what will it mean for everyone I'm in charge of if we don't succeed? And what about me? If I don't deliver in this role, am I setting myself up for failure as well? What's my way out of this if that happens?"

As he sat there pandering to his negative thoughts, lost again in his own doubts, there was a knock at the door.

"Come in," Joey said.

The company's mail carrier was standing there with an envelope for the young leader.

Joey looked down at the envelope. There was no return address, no stamp in the corner, nothing written except for his first name in perfect calligraphy and a label at the top marked URGENT.

He opened the envelope, pulled out a handwritten letter, and began to read it out loud:

Joey,

Thank you so much for the recommendation the other day.

After reflecting this weekend, I have decided that there was certainly merit in your suggestion that I work on avoiding startling those that I am currently serving.

I hope you have worked to cultivate that attitude of belief in yourself and your team these last few days.

Just know that it is a constant process. You must focus your efforts continuously if you want to see change.

It won't come easy, but it's worth it, and I have faith in you that, in time, it will become an everyday part of who you are.

I wanted to visit you today, but I have been summoned to an urgent LDL council meeting.

Please find the coin I intended to share with you inside this envelope.

I think it is of vital importance to you and your team to experience what this coin has to offer, but please be warned: this adventure is not for the faint of heart.

What you will see and hear and smell cannot be undone, so please, do not flip this coin until you are absolutely willing to experience what lies ahead.

Chaos, confusion, and calamity await, but don't be afraid, no harm will come to you.

I wish I could join you, but I know we will see each other again soon.

Your friend,
Marcus

Joey reached back into the envelope and pulled out the coin. If the old man had intended to enhance his sense of fear and uncertainty, he had succeeded.

He looked down to see the same **LDL** inscription on the back.

On the other side was some kind of metallic vessel, with the word Δέσμευση inscribed beneath.

As Joey turned the coin back and forth, a ship glittered brightly. It seemed as though it only appeared as he turned it over and disappeared once he turned it over again, but he couldn't be sure. Just as before, the coin was meticulously crafted, an artistic display representing an apparently dreadful experience.

As he prepared to flip the coin, Joey got butterflies in his stomach, the kind of nerves he had not experienced since his playing days.

He looked back at the letter and reread Marcus' warning. He looked down at the coin once more as he turned it between his fingers.

"Whatever is on the other side, it can't wait. If Marcus knows this is necessary for me and my team, I have to see it for myself."

Anxiety welled up inside him as he gave the coin a toss in the air. Once it fell back down, there was no denying that this was unlike anything the young leader had ever seen.

As he looked up, he quickly realized he was on the deck of a ship, probably the one from the coin, he assumed, and the ship was engaged in the kind of battle that one would only see in the movies.

He felt an immediate sensory overload.

His eyes surveyed the water immediately beyond the deck where he now stood.

There were almost continuous splashes behind the vessel, large shells just barely missing and sending colorful, dye-filled waves everywhere.

Through a cloud of smoke that seemed to come and go as the ship made its way through the water, he could see a line of other vessels, vastly larger than the one he was on, clearly taking aim at his tiny craft.

Beyond the smoke, he noticed a familiar sight. It was the Rising Sun Flag of Japan, waving atop the masts of the ships that were lobbing munitions his way. He focused in on what was taking place immediately in front of him.

It was complete, yet well-orchestrated, chaos.

There were guns firing forward and aft, men running all over the place, orders being bellowed, sirens blaring, and very quickly, Joey could feel fear.

It was not simply an emotion. He could actually feel it as though it was there in front of him and he could reach out and touch it. With his arms shaking and his knees trembling, he looked up to see the American flag flying high above him.

He could hear the guns, the blasts louder than anything he could recall. His eardrums were now in a constant state of ringing, only overtaken by the whistling sound of incoming projectiles.

He could make out gigantic shells headed directly toward him; the sailors on board were bracing themselves, not knowing if this was going to be the one that finally impacted their vessel.[1] A chaotic dance was taking place as they continued to close in on the Japanese vessels.

Joey wondered why they continued to head toward the enemy

---

1. Hornfischer, James D. *The Last Stand of the Tin Can Sailors: The Extraordinary World War II Story of the U.S. Navy's Finest Hour.* New York: Bantam Dell, 2004. Page 235.

rather than running away. They were clearly outmatched, the odds stacked unfavorably against them.

He wasn't sure if any other American support was nearby, but even someone with no military knowledge or experience could figure out the chances of this ending positively were not great.

Suddenly he heard a much deeper and heavier sound, and his whole body reverberated as he looked to the water to see the reason: three torpedoes had been launched toward the Japanese ships.

Immediately after launching their torpedoes at breakneck speed, the whole ship shaking as if she was outperforming her capabilities, the sailors turned the ship around as if to try and out-run the unfavorable odds.[2]

As they steamed away, Joey looked back to see flames rising dramatically into the air from one of the Japanese ships. The crew began to cheer, if only momentarily, at their successful strike.[3]

It didn't take long for him to realize that what might have been considered a tremendous success would be short-lived; this engagement had only just begun. Finally freed from paralyzing fear and uncertainty, Joey moved toward a gathering of sailors up ahead.

As he walked slowly and cautiously forward, he began to smell things he had never smelled. Diesel smoke, phosphorous fire, gunpowder, and burning metal filled his nostrils.

The ship continued to position itself for the next portion of its mission. Reaching the group of sailors, Joey determined rather quickly who the captain of the ship must be.

The man, clearly in charge, calmly ordered his men to prepare to engage the enemy cruiser ahead. He spoke to them about how their ship was all that stood between the Japanese cruiser and several American "jeep" carriers they were responsible for protecting.

---

2. Ibid, Page 254.
3. Ibid, Page 255.

That's what they intended to do, he said, though all they had left were the guns they were already engaging with.[4]

As they headed straight ahead for another giant Japanese vessel, their guns firing rapidly, impacting the enemy superstructure and wreaking havoc, Joey was in complete awe. He had no time to really consider what was taking place, but suddenly it became personal for him.

Looking at their faces, he could see they were terrified, yet they were doing everything in their power to carry out the task at hand. They were inflicting damage on an enemy significantly larger than themselves, defying the odds as shells whizzed over their heads and landed in between them and the carriers they were protecting.

Suddenly, though, the ship came to an immediate and sudden halt in the water. Joey snapped back to reality, the captain having ordered the engines "all back full" and the young leader saw the opposing Japanese ammunition making its way up the stern of their vessel and landing straight in front of them.

As the entire ship rattled and shook, he was thrown to the deck in front of him. The maneuver had worked, and Joey stood up, but as quickly as that had taken place, three enormous shells impacted the ship, throwing Joey back to the ground once more.[5]

Looking up, all his senses were immediately overtaken with the sights, smells, and sounds the explosions left in their wake.

He could hear the hissing of steam and the piercing screams. He could smell burning metal, and for the first time in his life, he could actually smell blood. But beyond the sounds and smells, it was the sight of the ship that made his knees buckle.

The entire aft part of the ship was in flames, having taken a brutal beating as the shells ripped through the stern. He could see shrapnel from the ship raining down below. Twisted metal,

---

4. Ibid, Page 286.
5. Ibid, Page 294.

the remnants of the blast, was scattered everywhere. White smoke from the asbestos insulation enveloped them.

Worst of all, he could see the injured and dead, bodies ripped apart, limbs torn off, and pools of blood interspersed with the rest of the carnage.[6]

Joey was now sick to his stomach, and his legs felt incapable of functioning. He reached into his pocket and felt the coin. He didn't think he could take this anymore.

As he pulled out the coin to send himself back to his office, away from the destruction and death he was witnessing, he heard another explosion at the back of the ship, and the coin went flying out of his hand.

Joey scrambled to retrieve the shiny object rolling across the deck in front of him. As he picked it up, locking it in a death grip between his fingers, he looked back out across the water and saw another American vessel sailing by, battered and beaten, its mast hanging down, with giant gaping holes littered from bow to stern.

This battle was clearly much bigger and important than what was taking place on his tiny ship, and he wondered what specific conflict they were immersed in, and what impact, if any, it had on the overall Allied effort in the Pacific theater of World War II, which most certainly was their location.

He got a full-scale glance of the enormous sacrifices being made as the ship sailed by. Back on his vessel, he overheard the captain give the abandon ship order, and it was clear to Joey that for them, the fight was over.[7]

Suddenly the ship became eerily quiet, its guns no longer firing, its boilers no longer producing steam. The captain ordered several of the remaining sailors to look for survivors.

Joey wasn't sure why or how, but he finally got the nerve to stand up, his legs finally capable of carrying him forward, and he followed one of the sailors toward the stern of the ship. He was no

---

6. Ibid, Page 233.
7. Ibid, Page 299.

longer grasping the coin, ready to flip it at a moment's notice. He wanted to see up close what these men had done for their country.

As they arrived at the back of the ship, the sailor he was following opened up the rear gun compartment to check for anyone who might have possibly survived.

The scene below literally took Joey's breath away.

The small compartment was full of blown up debris from the gun as well as bodies and body parts of the crew who served and died there.

Standing in the midst of it all was a man, barely alive, ripped apart from his neck to his waist, holding the final shell his gun had been unable to expend. He was delirious yet determined to fire the last round he was responsible for before he died. The sailor Joey had followed took the shell from the man and laid it next to him, turning his attention to retrieve another injured man from the wreckage.

When the sailor returned and opened the compartment for a second time, what transpired left Joey at a complete loss for words. His emotions finally getting the best of him, tears streamed down his face.

The critically injured man was attempting to stand again, cradling the shell and trying to do anything he could to load it back into the destroyed breech of his gun.

As Joey stood there in disbelief, the sailor retrieved the shell again, picked up the man and carried him out of the turret. He laid him down, and it was evident that the man no longer needed to worry about accomplishing his duty. He was finally at peace.[8]

Joey took one last glance around the ship, looking out into the waters where the survivors began to gather as they awaited either rescue or capture, and he wiped the tears from his face.

He burned in his mind the image of the sinking vessel, how

8. Ibid, Page 332.

valiantly its crew had fought, and the dedication he had just seen firsthand from the man in the aft turret.

He tossed the coin into the air, the ship emblazoned on its face flickering back and forth as it spun back down. Joey collapsed on the floor of his office, completely overcome with what he had just experienced.

"Joey? Joey, are you alright?"

Joey wasn't sure, but he sensed that he must have passed out as soon as he arrived back in his office. As he came to, he heard the quiet, familiar voice he was growing accustomed to. Marcus knelt next to him, grasping Joey's shoulder and helping him to stand up.

"Here, drink some water," Marcus said, handing Joey a glass.

"What happened?" the young leader asked.

"You've been out of it for a couple of minutes," the old man responded.

"It's an overwhelming experience, I know."

"You can say that again. I think it was one of those life-altering moments I'll never forget," Joey said, struggling to choose the right words.

His mind was swirling with thoughts, and he was still reeling from what he had experienced, but he also was curious about how Marcus had gotten into his office. He set that aside for the time being, deciding instead to focus on the lingering questions from his journey.

"Can you fill in the gaps for me about what I just encountered?" he asked. "And why was it so important that it couldn't wait until you got here?"

"I'm sorry about that. I had an urgent **LDL** council meeting to attend, and I wasn't sure how long it would last. You know how those kinds of meetings tend to go, I'm sure. Plus, if I'm being honest, I hate being on ships. I spent my whole Navy career trying to avoid them."

The honesty with which Marcus explained himself made Joey chuckle, the humor serving as a brief recess from the emotions still vividly at the forefront of his mind. He still wasn't sure what the **LDL** Council was, having failed to ask his mentor about the consistent inscription on the coins to this point, but now didn't seem like the time.

"Joey, you were just a witness to the crew of the USS *Samuel B. Roberts*, a destroyer escort filled with some of the most heroic men the United States has ever sent to war. They were fighting valiantly during the Battle off Samar, an absolutely critical part of the overall Battle of Leyte Gulf, one of the largest naval battles in the history of the world.

"The Japanese had drawn up a plan, called Sho-Go 1, which was predicated on an ability to lure away ADM "Bull" Halsey's Third Fleet with a decoy group of aircraft carriers, thereby exposing the U.S. landing force in the Philippines under General Douglas MacArthur to attack from multiple sides. Halsey took the bait and left behind RADM Clifton Sprague and one of his Task Forces, known as Taffy 3, to defend itself against the oncoming Japanese onslaught from Admiral Takeo Kurita, who had appeared to retreat from the battle earlier before turning around and catching Taffy 3 by surprise.

"Taffy 3, consisting of thirteen warships made up of six 'jeep' carriers, three 'tin can' destroyers, and four destroyer escorts, would go up against Japan's Center Force, an adversary they had no business attempting to do battle with. The Japanese had four enormous battleships, one of which, the *Yamato*, weighed by itself almost exactly the same as all thirteen of Taffy 3's ships combined.[9] If that wasn't bad enough, the Japanese Force had six heavy cruisers, two light cruisers, and eleven destroyers that Taffy 3 would have to contend with as well. It wasn't just that their chances were slim. It was, as LCDR Robert Copeland, Commanding Officer of the *Sammy B* (who you just saw leading his crew until the bitter end), put it before the battle began: 'This will

---

9. Ibid, Page 165.

be a fight against overwhelming odds from which survival cannot be expected. We will do what damage we can.'[10]

"They knew rather quickly that there was no expectation of survival, that help was not coming, and that the decision to engage the enemy was one that would never be recommended in any war-gaming scenario by any sane individual. However, what took place on the morning of October 25, 1944, was one of the greatest upsets in naval history."

"Wait, they won?" Joey shouted, reluctant to believe that after what he had seen, there was any way they could have come out on top.

"It is hard to say that anyone wins in a situation like that, with the United States losing two escort carriers, two destroyers, and the *Samuel B. Roberts* in the process," Marcus replied. "But the brave men of Taffy 3 caused such chaos and confusion in their courageous attacks on the superior Japanese force that Admiral Kurita decided to retreat, ultimately unsure of the size and scope of the foe he was facing.

"When it was all said and done at Leyte Gulf, the Japanese Navy had suffered its final major defeat of World War II, thanks in no small part to the willingness of Taffy 3 to sail into harm's way, fully anticipating their sacrifice in the process."

"That's incredible!" Joey exclaimed. "But I'm still a little confused. Why would they even go into battle if they knew it was one they had no chance of winning? Why sacrifice your men and your ships?" The memory of what he just witnessed was still so distinctly etched in his mind that he couldn't wrap his head around the necessity of the engagement.

"Because it was much bigger than just them," Marcus declared. "That was the mindset of those men. They lived their lives with the understanding that IT'S NOT ABOUT YOU, and it never will be. For them, it was about the three Ms: the Mission, the

---

10. Ibid, Page 150.

Men, Me. They were in that order, never to be reprioritized or altered. The men were mission-focused, and the mission stated that their duty was to engage the enemy and protect their carriers. Just because the necessity of the engagement was immensely clear to them, though, doesn't mean they weren't terrified of what was taking place."

"I could feel that deep down in my soul," Joey said, interrupting Marcus. "Fear was present, but even though they were afraid, they didn't stay scared, and they certainly didn't run away from their responsibilities or shirk their duty. They continued to operate the way they had prepared, the intensity of the moment never derailing them from doing everything in their power to inflict as much damage as humanly possible."[11]

"Exactly! At that moment, self-preservation went out the window because the standards they operated from were based on the value of commitment: commitment to the greater purpose worth fighting for, commitment to each other, and an individual commitment to acting in a way that demonstrated what they represented.

"I think we misunderstand what it means to be committed. Commitment isn't just being *all in* some of the time. It isn't just doing the work when it's easy. It isn't helping out just when we stand to gain something. It isn't being a team player just when it serves our interests. Commitment is being *all in, all the time.*

"Unfortunately, we miss the mark on this far too often today. Everyone is always looking for a plan B or wondering where the back door is if things don't work out exactly as they intended.

"There was no plan B for the *Sammy B*. Those men knew what was at stake, and their actions were simply a reflection of their commitment to each other and their country."

Marcus paused for a moment, and then went on. "You know, I've made two very public commitments in my life, moments that

---

11. Ibid, Page 286.

were watched by friends and family and celebrated for what they represented. When I married my late wife and we committed to spending the rest of our lives together, for better or for worse, for rich or for poor, in sickness and in health, I didn't do it conditionally based on whether or not my wife was going to serve my own interests or on what I would personally gain from that commitment. I did it out of love; I was focused on doing everything in my power to serve her, regardless of whether or not it was reciprocated every moment of every day.

"And when I took my Oath of Office, committing to support and defend the Constitution of the United States against all enemies, foreign and domestic, I didn't commit to doing so up to a certain point. I did so with the understanding that, just like so many of the men of Taffy 3, it was possible my commitment would mean the ultimate sacrifice. There was no fine print, no other alternatives."

Looking intently at Joey, Marcus said, "You've made a pretty big public commitment yourself."

"I have?"

"Of course! I'm sure when you made the commitment to play basketball, you had a big signing day celebration, surrounded by family and friends recognizing you for your accomplishment."

"Oh yeah, my high school went all out to show me how proud they were!"

"I'm also sure that at that moment, as a high school kid, you weren't thinking about the gassers, the early morning practices, or the devastating buzzer-beating losses that would come with that commitment. You weren't thinking about what your next option would be if the coach didn't give you the playing time you thought you deserved or things didn't go your way. You were simply focused on the fact that, through your hard work, you had earned a scholarship.

"But it was about so much more than just getting a scholarship. It was a declaration of your commitment to be a part of something bigger than yourself. It was about your commitment to your future teammates and your future university. It was about representing yourself in a way that would reflect properly on your program, and you continue to be that representative, even today.

"I believe that with that commitment, you have an obligation. You have an obligation to those that laid the foundation for you and your program, to those that you would get the opportunity to play with for four years and ultimately lead as a team captain, and to those that would come after you. You have an obligation to be committed to doing everything in your power to add to your team's legacy and leave your program in a better place than where you found it. And that kind of commitment is about more than just what happens on the court. That level of commitment, to leave that kind of mark, is about who you are in every aspect of your life.

"Look, Joey, here's the point. You've made great progress these last few weeks. I admire you for the introspection, the ability to articulate your values and turn them into standards that your team can operate from. I commend you for continuing to work to find your purpose, and for creating a vision that your team can collectively believe in. I respect you for making a dedicated effort to create that sense of belief, and for making the hard decision not to sacrifice quality for a quick buck.

"But I also know that you continue to look for your way out, and I'm here to tell you that attempting to have one foot in the door and one foot out won't work. If you don't jump in with both feet, if you don't actually commit yourself to this team, then you can't possibly expect them to give it their all for you in return. You see, son, there aren't levels of commitment. You can't be a little committed, half committed, or mostly committed. By the definition of the word and what it means to live it out daily, either you *are* committed or you *aren't*. And you *need* to be committed to this team. This must become a part of who you are, become so ingrained that you can't even fathom another alternative."

"Like the man in the aft turret!" Joey exclaimed. "He was the most committed person I think I have ever seen. He was doing everything in his power to get that last round off, to accomplish his mission, even though he knew he wasn't going to make it." The young leader's voice trembled as he recalled the heroic effort he had witnessed.

"I was hoping you were going to find your way back there," Marcus responded. "Yes, Paul Henry Carr was the epitome of commitment. He was committed to leading his team in the operation of Gun 52 with a standard of excellence and unwavering devotion to duty. What you didn't see—what we often don't get to see—is the preparation that comes with commitment, and the accountability necessary to create a culture where everyone is operating with that same commitment to excellence. Paul Henry Carr was meticulous in his care of Gun 52. He worked day in and day out to ensure that his team was deliberate and intentional in its preparation, in its commitment to operating with the proper standards, and it showed. LCDR Copeland even went so far as to claim that Gun 52 was one of the best that had ever existed in the US Navy.[12]

"That commitment to being the best they were capable of manifested itself on the morning of October 25th, as Gun 52 was able to expend 324 rounds of five-inch shells in just thirty-five minutes. Paul Henry Carr's team fired with such efficiency, such calmness, and such accuracy that they took on an enemy ship over twelve times their weight and held their own. Even after losing power to the turret and disabling the automatic gas ejection system for the ammunition, they continued to fire, getting off seven or eight more rounds while having to manually eject the shells, before one finally cooked off in the breech, creating the explosion that ultimately mortally wounded Mr. Carr. And even after all of that, he continued to personify what commitment truly means when he refused to succumb to his injuries without attempting to fire that last shell he was responsible for.[13]

---

12. Ibid, Page 288.
13. Ibid, Page 332.

"Joey, your commitment may never take that form, but the lessons learned from Paul Henry Carr can create in you the desire to habituate that same understanding of what it takes to lead, and what can happen when a team of individuals is *all in, all the time.*"

Marcus gave his young protege a hug, retrieved his coin, and walked out the door. He was confident that Joey was capable of taking the next step forward, and he believed deeply that the young man was well on his way to being the type of leader his team so desperately needed.

CHAPTER 5
Κίνητρο
MOTIVATION

"People often say that motivation doesn't last. Well, neither does bathing—that's why we recommend it daily."

—Zig Ziglar

JOEY SAT QUIETLY for a few moments as he continued to process the intensity of what he had just experienced. He was emotionally exhausted, and it wasn't even lunchtime yet. He pondered everything Marcus had shared with him, his thoughts continuously drifting back to the aft gun turret and Paul Henry Carr.

What would it take for me to be committed like that? he wondered. There was no doubt in his mind that the old man was correct—that level of commitment isn't something that just comes naturally. It is cultivated over time, a continuous process of choosing the team and its purpose over selfish desires.

For Paul Henry Carr, it had become second nature, almost like breathing. There was no other alternative, no exit strategy, no backup plan. He had achieved a level of commitment Joey could hardly fathom.

I've spent my whole life focused on what I stood to gain from every experience and leadership opportunity I have been afforded, Joey thought. *When I was named Class President, I was excited because it would help me get into a good school. When I secured a schol-*

arship, I was thrilled because of what I thought the coaching staff would provide me in my four years. When I got this assignment, all I could think about was that corner office two stories up. Self-preservation and self-gratification have been barriers to me understanding what it truly means to be committed to something.

Right then and there, he made a decision to do better.

He would take the time to consider his actions and determine whether they were in alignment with the value of commitment that he had just seen displayed. He would assess whether or not he was living out what he now knew deep down to be true.

As his thoughts turned from self to his team, he quickly realized that some of them shared the same struggles he was facing.

He wasn't sure if anyone on the team was really committed, but he knew for sure that Sam was falling short and missing the mark, and he felt that Liz might be in the same boat as well.

They both had influence over other members of the team and were important, in his mind, to establishing a standard of commitment moving forward.

How could I possibly convey what I just witnessed to them? he wondered. Joey knew there was no way his words could do justice to the experience, and besides, the team would think he had absolutely gone crazy if he tried to explain Marcus and the coins to them. Without a doubt, they would think he had broken under the enormous pressure he was facing and would have him committed immediately for psychological evaluations. He began to laugh as he thought about how preposterous the whole thing was.

Time travel.

Magic coins.

An old man who had a habit of appearing out of nowhere and disappearing before he could bat an eye.

It was insane.

If he hadn't felt it down in the depths of his soul, and if he hadn't seen it all with his own two eyes, he wouldn't believe it to be true either.

He needed a way to convince the team that he was committed, and he wanted to be able to inspire them to embrace the same level of commitment in their own lives.

Joey then made what he considered to be the natural, rational decision in such a circumstance: he opened a web browser and searched for "motivational speech," pulling up video after video. He scrolled through millions of results, looking for the right message to share.

Just then, there was a knock at his office, the handle turning and door opening before he had a chance to look up.

Marcus strolled back into the room.

Joey perked up when he saw him, hopeful that he was about to receive some more wisdom that he could pass on to his team.

"Hey, sorry...I got all the way down to the garage and realized I didn't get my parking ticket validated. They sent me back up here to your office to get someone to take care of it," Marcus said, with the sly grin Joey was growing accustomed to.

"Angela can take care of that for you right out there," the young leader replied, pointing to the administrative assistant sitting out in the hall, his face noticeably dejected at the insignificant request.

"Thanks! Those rates are just brutal around here at this time of day," Marcus responded, before catching the look on Joey's face.

"Hey, I was thinking on the ride down the elevator that I wished we had talked a little more about something before I left," he continued, Joey's countenance brightening yet again at the prospect of another journey.

Marcus walked back over to the desk and leaned across, catching a glimpse of the motivational speeches lining Joey's computer screen. "What's all this?" he asked, curious as to why his young companion would need any more material in the aftermath of his morning trip to the South Pacific.

"It's just...I'm not sure how I can explain this all to my team," Joey blurted out. "All these experiences have done wonders for me in just a few short weeks, but how do I translate them into motivation for everyone else? They couldn't begin to understand what you've shown me, and I don't think I've got it in me to provide them with enough pep talks to keep them going. Some of them seem to feel that if it's not impacting their wallets or showing up on their performance reviews, it's not worth getting excited about."

"And what about you?" Marcus inquired. "What is going to sustain you through the daily grind and stress associated with your situation? Where do you find your motivation?"

"I guess, lately, that's been coming from you," Joey replied. "Every time we get together, I leave reinvigorated, excited about the future, and challenged to become a better leader. I just want to provide the same thing for them."

"That's admirable, and I'm really glad that your focus is on how you can help them, but I think you're looking at it all wrong. Here, scroll down the page and let's watch one of these videos, and I'll show you what I mean."

"Don't you have another coin we could use instead?" Joey asked, hoping that another adventure awaited the two of them.

"Sure, I've got a coin for just about anything," Marcus explained, "but I'm not allowed to take anyone on two trips in the same day. **LDL** rules, I'm afraid."

"What is **LDL** anyway?" Joey asked. He had been wanting to ask Marcus about this; maybe now was the right moment to bring it up.

"Leaders Developing Leaders!" Marcus exclaimed. "It's an ancient organization. Been around for centuries. We've helped many a young person like yourself navigate the challenges of leadership, passing on time-tested principles of how to be successful to those who have what we are looking for."

"How do you get to become a member of the group?" Joey asked.

"I'm afraid a referral from another member of the **LDL** team is the only way to be selected. And, you have to earn your coin. No exceptions!" Marcus responded firmly.

"How did you earn your coin?"

"A right place at the right time situation for sure, but that's another story for another day."

Marcus took the mouse from Joey, shifting the conversation back to the task at hand as he selected a video to make his point. "Here, this should be right up your alley!"

Joey looked down at the description: *Jim Valvano-Cutting Down the Nets.* The old man was correct. The late, great Jimmy V, former head coach of the North Carolina State men's basketball program and 1983 National Champion, was one of the best.

Joey secretly wished Marcus had a coin that would take them to that Championship win over Houston, one of the greatest games in college basketball history, so he could see Lorenzo Charles grab a last-second heave out of mid-air and drop it in the basket as time expired to secure the victory for the Wolfpack.

Marcus didn't say a word as Coach Valvano started to talk, letting Joey listen intently to what the man had to say.

As the young leader absorbed the beginning of Jimmy's talk that day to the Million Dollar Round Table, he thought through everything he knew about the man.

The Championship.

The battle with cancer.

The ESPYS speech.

The V Foundation for Cancer Research.

The legacy he left behind.

The man was a gifted speaker, full of life, and brimming with passion.

If I could harness just a little bit of that myself, Joey thought, *I'm sure I could get through to my team.*

It didn't take long for Joey to pick up on a familiar tone and language. Coach Valvano talked about his dream of winning a National Championship, emphasizing that "nothing happens without a dream first."[1]

He shared a heart-wrenching story about the first time he made the NCAA Basketball tournament at Iona, losing in the first round and then going home to his parents' house in New York. His father took Coach Valvano up to his bedroom and pointed at a suitcase on the floor, telling his son "My bags are packed. When you make it to the National Championship, I'll be there."

Jim tried to let his dad know how hard it was to make it to the title game, but his dad just repeated, "You'll get there; I know you will. And when you do, my bags are packed."[2]

For Coach Valvano, this was "the gift [his] father gave [him]," the belief he had in him before he had it in himself, and so he tried to do the same with his players. He decided early on, "I've got to be the first believer."[3]

He talked about how his dad's level of belief was the reason, even though the man never had any real authority or position, that he was able to influence more people than anyone he had ever met.

He talked about meeting Bob Richards as a kid. Mr. Richards, a two-time Olympic pole vault champion, told him that the Lord must have loved ordinary people because he made so many of them. He continued by shouting, "Every single day, in every walk of life, ordinary people do extraordinary things!"[4]

For Coach Valvano, that became connected to his purpose. He was an ordinary man who wanted to do extraordinary things in his life. He shared stories of incredible vision—for instance, taking an entire practice each season with no balls and no whistles. All that was on the court was a ladder and some scissors. The team would spend the day practicing "cutting down the nets," a symbolic gesture of what could become reality: the team hoisting each other on their shoulders, celebrating a National Championship.

---

1. Holladay, Daniel. "Jimmy V-Cutting Down the Nets." Online video clip.
   Youtube. 14 Mar 2017.
2. Ibid.
3. Ibid.
4. Ibid.

Coach Valvano showed his team what the dream was; he laid out the vision for them so clearly they could actually see it themselves, and then he went about putting in the work to make the dream become a reality.

Purpose, dreams, vision, belief, and commitment—Joey could pinpoint them all. This was a man who had put into practice the things Marcus had been sharing with him over the last several weeks. But more than that, it was Valvano's energy level and the passion with which he spoke that had Joey ready to run through a brick wall.

Next Coach Valvano laid out his formula for how he remained at the top of a competitive field. "YOU plus MOTIVATION equals SUCCESS," he explained. He believed that motivation was the key to success, and Joey was finding it difficult to disagree with him.

"Now *this* is a speech," he exclaimed to Marcus.

Coach Valvano went on to say that it takes motivation to go from ordinary to extraordinary, and that to him, motivation consisted of three things: enthusiasm, dreams, and work ethic.[5] He quoted Ralph Waldo Emerson, stating that "nothing great was ever achieved without enthusiasm."[6] He asked the audience, "How enthusiastic are you every day in your profession?"

Joey took that question like a punch to the gut. He knew how hard it had been for him to find enthusiasm each day. When he felt that collective purpose being established, he could sense his enthusiasm increasing, but as soon as it went up, it seemed to crash right back down. His emotions were running high and low, in sync with the ups and downs of the work week.

Coach Valvano spoke about how the relationship between work ethic and success was not direct. "It's not if you work hard, you will be successful. It's if you don't work hard, you've got no shot."[7]

5. Ibid.
6. Ibid.

Joey had never considered that line of thinking before. He had always been taught that you work harder than everyone else so that you can become successful. He tucked that in the back of his mind as he brought his attention back to how to motivate his team.

What struck him the most was the moment Jimmy V told the group that he had never in twenty-one years motivated anyone "except one person, James Thomas Anthony Valvano."[8] It was a full-time job keeping himself where he needed to be, and he hoped that when he was at that level, others would follow suit.

As the talk ended, Joey was left pondering that simple idea.

How could he say he didn't motivate anyone else? Of course he did. I was motivated just listening to him, the young leader thought to himself.

He looked over at Marcus, suddenly realizing that this whole thing was a setup.

"You didn't just pick a video at random, did you?" he asked the old man.

Marcus looked at Joey, giving him a glance clearly indicating that his young protégé was onto him. "There is no random with me!" he proclaimed. "Everything is done at the appropriate time for the appropriate reason."

"So, why this video then? Because I'm a basketball guy?"

"Yes, but also because I think Coach Valvano can teach us several important lessons, and we didn't need a coin to get us there! What stood out to you from his talk?"

"I guess the biggest thing was how much what he said connected to our previous discussions on purpose, dreams, vision, and belief," Joey answered. "But then he told the audience that he didn't motivate anyone but himself. That's where he lost me. He was one of the most motivational coaches of his time."

"Those are all great observations. You probably already know

---

7. Ibid.
8. Ibid.

what I'm going to ask you next then," Marcus said, smiling because he could tell Joey was starting to pick up on his rhythm.

"I'll just go ahead and answer it for you," Joey responded. "My motivation lately has come from seeing everyone begin to connect their own individual purposes to the collective purpose of our team. That has invigorated me, and the more I have gotten to know my team, the more enthusiastic I have been about what we are setting out to accomplish together. But as I told you, I've also been relying on our trips together to inspire me. It seems that every time I feel like I'm on my way to understanding what I need to do to lead this team, something happens that brings me back to reality or makes me question the direction we are headed."

"Do you think that pressure is going to subside any time soon?" Marcus asked. "Do you think that the higher up you go and the more people you lead, the easier it becomes to stay motivated? The pressure is going to continue to be there, the distractions are going to increase, and the responsibilities are going to continue to surge. Where you want to go as a leader requires you to move beyond looking everywhere else for motivation. You need to find a way to provide that for yourself, just like Coach Valvano."

"How do I do that?" Joey asked, sounding unconvinced.

"First, you need to understand why people are really motivated in the first place," Marcus replied.

"It seems like the promise of bonuses or the fear of reprisal works pretty well," Joey said sarcastically.

"Sure, you can use 'the carrot and the stick' model, offering extrinsic rewards or punishments as motivation for accomplishing tasks, but those simply drive task accomplishment for task accomplishment's sake. It's not that extrinsic motivators are bad. In fact, we all rely on them to one degree or another. They can be effective when used properly. But what people really need is to find that intrinsic connection that sustains them when the extrinsic motivators aren't present or have to be removed. And that's done through the things Coach Valvano spoke about to the Million Dollar Round Table that afternoon.

"Motivation is directly connected to purpose, to the vision, and to individual ownership of that collective dream. When you can provide an individual connection to collective purpose, when people sense the need for their role and its importance in making the purpose come to fruition, and when they feel that what they do actually matters, they will be motivated to contribute to the team. Everyone wants to feel that sense of accomplishment, a connection to meaningful work. They want to know that where you are taking them will lead to them becoming the best version of themselves. When you do that, you can inspire them from the inside out."

Joey thought for a second. The idea of different types of motivation wasn't all that foreign to him. He had experienced this his entire life in athletics.

Make the time on the sprints to avoid more sprints.

Stay in the coach's good graces if you want to see the court.

He also knew the intrinsic feeling of playing a part in something bigger than himself. That's what he loved about team sports. Together they could accomplish more than they could on their own.

"So, keep driving home the vision and keep connecting purpose to the dream. That's how I motivate the team?" he asked.

Marcus nodded. "Yes, you should do those things. But you also need to fully understand what Coach Valvano meant when he said he only worried about motivating himself. If you can't motivate yourself, Joey, how can you possibly expect to motivate others? It's not just about setting an inspirational example; you also must be working on becoming a person who is enthusiastic, who has habituated a process of self-motivation to the point that it becomes an inseparable part of who you are as a leader.

"Fall back on your purpose, remind yourself continuously of the vision, don't be afraid to dream big dreams, set realistic goals that can be measured and used as small surges of motivation along the way, become an over-believer, and be committed to the pursuit of it all and to the team. You get yourself to a Jimmy V-level of self-motivation by focusing on those things."

"I still don't get why he would say he didn't motivate anyone else though," Joey reiterated.

"Oh, Jim Valvano motivated others; there is no doubt about that. He still does to this day. It's hard to watch his ESPYs speech and not become emotional. I still get chills when he tells the audience 'Don't give up. Don't ever give up.'[9]

"But it wasn't because he was focused on how inspirational he was that he was so inspirational. The inspiration just became an outward expression of an inward process of cultivating self-motivation in his own life, of becoming the person he knew he could be. It was simply an extension of who he was as a man. Coach Valvano lived out his recipe for success daily. It wasn't just a keynote speech or a talk in the locker room. He was enthusiastic until the very end. He never stopped dreaming. He never stopped working as hard as he could to realize his purpose of being extraordinary in life."

"But I'm not Coach Valvano. I don't communicate in that way, and I'm not sure I ever could," Joey said before Marcus could continue.

"Good! No one is asking you to be Jimmy V, son. He wouldn't want that for you anyway. He knew he needed to be authentic and stay true to himself as a leader, even when other coaches in his league didn't like his style or approach. Coach Valvano knew that all of us are motivated differently. He knew that we all have our own hopes, our own dreams, and our own beliefs. Jimmy V was intentional about how he impacted each and every person in his life, and because he was able to figure out what each player needed and what they brought to the team, he was able to connect them to the overall purpose and add meaning to their lives.

---

9. The V Foundation for Cancer Research. "Jim's 1993 ESPY Speech." Online video clip. Youtube. 28 Sep 2008.

"Here's what it all boils down to with self-motivation, Joey. All of these experiences and adventures are great, but we can't live our lives half-time speech to half-time speech, waiting on the next big moment to come along and motivate us again. That doesn't mean there isn't a place for those mountaintop experiences we've shared together recently.

"Mountaintops are important to the human race, after all. If you are Jewish, you believe Moses received the Ten Commandments from a mountaintop. If you are Christian, you believe Jesus gave his most famous sermon from a mountain. If you are a follower of Islam, you believe Muhammad received his first revelation from on top of a mountain. If you are Hindu, you believe Shiva abides on the top of a mountain.

"You should experience as many mountaintop moments as possible. You should soak up the half-time speeches when they occur. Finding words of wisdom and taking inspiration from these moments is important, and you will need them to be prepared to step into that role for your team when necessary, but they won't sustain you during the grind in the game of life, because *we* don't live *our* lives on the mountaintop. We live, we work, we spend our time, and we operate out of the valley.

"And in order to live in the valley, in order to survive the daily challenges that are thrown your way, you need to prepare yourself with a habit of self-motivation, working consistently to keep yourself at a level worth emulating so you can lead effectively, while keeping the guideposts from the mountains in your sight as long as possible.

"There will come a time, however, when you can no longer see the markers, when the fog of life obscures the mountaintop. It happens to us all. It's in those moments when we start to forget what is important that we need to journey back up the mountain and rediscover those guideposts, the values that drive everything in our lives. But we can't live our lives climbing up and down the mountain. We have to be able to sustain ourselves in the valley—because that's where the fight is!"

Joey, as always, was appreciative of Marcus and the time he had spent with him, and he knew that he still had much to learn from his mentor, but he sensed that this was his cue to step out on his own and begin to operate from a place of self-reliance.

He enveloped Marcus in a hug, grabbed his parking ticket, and walked to Angela's desk outside his office and stamped it himself. He placed it in Marcus' hand, the gesture making clear that this was a turning point for him in his leadership journey, and he watched as Marcus made his way to the elevator and disappeared out of sight.

He turned back toward his office, summoning everyone into the conference room in the process. It was well into the afternoon, and Joey felt emotionally spent between his journey to the South Pacific and the realization that the responsibility for self-motivation fell squarely on his shoulders.

He looked at the group. The expressions on their faces made it evident that it had been another day of frustration without much progress. He decided that he would put into practice the example he had just learned from Coach Valvano as he tried to inspire a new level of motivation and commitment moving forward.

He would show them the vision clearly and put the purpose before them in a tangible way.

"Tomorrow," he said, "We're going to take a little trip!"

CHAPTER 6
Παιδεία
DISCIPLINE

"Being busy does not mean real work...seeming to do is not doing."

—Thomas Edison

T HE PREVIOUS DAY had led Joey to another moment of clarity. He wanted to demonstrate his commitment, he wanted to communicate its importance to his team, and he wanted to do so in a way that the team could reach out and touch it.

The young leader wanted them to be inspired in the same way he had been inspired by the men of the *Samuel B. Roberts,* to see the vision as clearly as Jimmy V's team could see it when they practiced cutting down the nets.

He wanted to create a mountaintop experience for his team that would provide them with guideposts they could look back on as they continued to grind through life in the valley that was the business district of downtown Atlanta.

He had spent the rest of his afternoon trying to set up the next day's adventures, making a series of phone calls in hopes of connecting the purpose to the dream for his team.

It was a last-minute decision he hoped would pay off in the long run, pulling the group away from a day of work for what amounted to little more than a company field trip.

As everyone met in the parking garage the next morning and

crammed into a company van, Joey still had given them no indication of where they were headed.

He wanted to keep the suspense going as long as possible,
merely telling them all to pack a lunch and expect to spend the
entire day away from their desks.

This had been met with anticipated skepticism. The team was
already struggling with a lack of productivity and results, and to
take an entire day away for a field trip would certainly not do
anything to curb their anxiety over the lack of solutions they had
come up with to this point.

Joey simply asked for trust.

He was OK with the skepticism, telling himself that he would
feel the same way if he was in their shoes. Still, if something like
this had worked for Coach Valvano, maybe it could work for him
too.

Joey drove the van out of the parking garage and began to
make his way down Interstate 75, heading south toward Robins
Air Force Base where they would be spending their day.

The two-hour drive was important for several reasons.

It would provide the team with an opportunity to get to know
each other outside of work, hopefully in a way that would allow
them to continue to forge bonds with each other that would be
needed down the road. Joey used the time driving down to continue fostering a deeper relationship with them, talking further
about their lives and families, cracking jokes, and allowing his
authenticity to shine through as Marcus had suggested.

The trip wasn't just about bonding as a team, though.

They were headed to Robins Air Force Base because it was
one of the numerous installations across the country that used the
products his team was trying so desperately to salvage. The base
was home to the largest single-site industrial complex in the state
of Georgia, providing planned maintenance for all aircraft in a
variety of platforms for the United States Air Force.

The men and women who worked at Robins were responsible
for repairing and upgrading thousands of aircraft each year, and

the part his team was working so hard to manufacture without sacrificing an ounce of quality was one of thousands of parts installed in these aircraft as they were being maintained.

Everyone on the team understood that they were responsible for just one small part in a much larger plan, one aircraft component that must work together with thousands of others, but Joey hoped that showing them firsthand what their work was leading to would have an impact on them the way so many of his recent journeys had on him.

They pulled up to the gate, and the military police searched the van. The base was on heightened security, and the team knew pretty quickly that where they were headed would be much different than the standard day in their cubicles on the twenty-third floor.

The van was directed to a hangar on the far side of the airfield. A member of the Warner Robins Air Logistics Complex was outside to greet them, introducing herself as the unit's Public Affairs Officer and their tour guide for the day.

Immediately Joey could sense a pep in his team's step. They were in awe at the number of aircraft being repaired in the facility, taken aback at just how large of an operation it was to get each "bird" back up and flying missions in support of the country's interests at home and abroad.

The team was given the opportunity to walk around, ask questions, see fighter jets, reconnaissance aircraft, transport aircraft, special operations helicopters, and more.

Joey couldn't help thinking how much Marcus would have enjoyed this experience, being able to relive his flying days in the Navy and more than likely giving a good ribbing to his Air Force counterparts.

If the tour of the aircraft and the facilities weren't enough to convince the team of the small but significant role they were playing, the chance to meet a group of pilots from the 413th Flight Test Group solidified it. It connected that purpose directly to their dream of meeting production goals without sacrificing quality.

Joey could see it in their eyes.

They hung on every word as the pilots explained to them that before any of the aircraft here could be sent back out to the units across the country who would use them, they had to certify them as safe for flight.

They piloted aircraft every single day that were not safe to fly in order to verify that all the maintenance work had been completed properly and each aircraft was ready to return to operational use.

The team could hardly fathom the responsibilities of testing aircraft in extreme flight regimes to make sure they were safe as the pilots explained what a functional check flight involved. Any little thing could be wrong or go wrong, and it was up to the pilots to be able to identify at a moment's notice when something was not working properly, diagnose it on the spot, and get the aircraft landed back safely for more work to be done.

They did the same thing over and over again, each day spent living on the edge of continuous uncertainty.

Suddenly Joey's team could see that this was not just about numbers and the bottom line anymore. There were real people connected to their work, the faces of eager young men and women in flight suits who were prepared to take what they provided up in the air and test it out.

The day was going exactly as Joey had hoped it would.

As they finished the tour, the team moved on to the flight line to watch as aircraft prepared to take off and land. For some members of the team, it was an emotional moment.

Joey took the opportunity at hand to ask one of the maintenance workers to bring him one of the parts his team was working so hard to produce. He held it up for everyone to see as he tried his best to connect the emotional dots that they all were feeling.

He spoke once again of purpose, weaving as many of their individual purposes as possible into his understanding of their collective purpose of providing "what was needed to those who needed it when they needed it."

He reaffirmed his dream of doing that without sacrificing quality.

He spoke about how this whole experience represented the vision, the importance of what they were doing on full display for them to see as a fighter jet roared overhead.

He spoke about the standards they would have to operate with in order to make the vision a reality.

He talked once more about his belief in this team because of his belief in each one of them individually.

And he affirmed for them yet again his commitment to what they were trying to accomplish.

He promised them he would do everything he could to help them succeed, but he asked them for the same level of commitment in return.

He told them he knew this wouldn't happen overnight, but he was prepared to fight every day to see it realized.

Joey finished by saying that from this moment forward they would get his very best, that he would bring a relentless enthusiasm each day he was their leader, and that he hoped over time they would come to realize the importance of doing the same.

Joey could sense the tide shifting as they walked back off the flight line into the hangar and said their goodbyes, thanking everyone for showing them the importance of what they were doing for them from a skyscraper in downtown Atlanta.

The ride home was much quieter.

There was a deep introspection taking place among the team, and Joey got the feeling that maybe, just maybe, they were finally starting to come together and fully embrace the challenge before them.

The rest of the week brought a new energy level to the twenty-third floor. Everyone seemed enthusiastic, working hard individually and collectively to find a solution.

Even Sam and Liz put in an increased effort. Whether that was a result of not wanting to look bad in front of the rest of the team or because they had truly bought into what the group was doing was up for debate, but regardless, Joey was pleased to see them integrating nicely with everyone else.

He sensed that a breakthrough was coming—that they would finally be moving toward discovering a solution.

That feeling was short-lived, however.

As he was preparing to gather his belongings for his drive home on Friday afternoon, excited at the prospect of what was taking place and what next week would bring, his phone rang.

It was the twenty-fifth-floor secretary. The board of directors was holding an impromptu meeting on Monday morning, and his presence was being requested to give an update on where they stood.

Just when it seemed that his team was poised to succeed, he knew he would be grilled on what was taking so long and why they were going to fall short of quarterly projections.

Joey felt numb.

The rest of the team had already departed for the weekend, and he knew that he would need their help preparing to answer to the board before Monday, but he also didn't want them spending the weekend away from their families for his sake.

Joey decided he would wait to notify the team until Saturday evening. He would let them know that he would be spending Sunday afternoon at the office preparing for the meeting, and he outlined a few numbers and documents he needed from them, but he would let them know he had no expectation of them spending their Sunday with him on the twenty-third floor.

His mindset was slowly shifting from himself toward them, more concerned about what they needed and what he could do to help them than what would happen to him Monday morning.

The mission still remained at the forefront of what they were trying to do, though.

The Mission, the Men, Me, he reminded himself. *The Mission, the Men,* then *Me.*

Monday would arrive regardless of whether he wanted it to or not, and there was no point fretting over it right then and there, so Joey decided to spend the next twenty-four hours focused on his own rest.

He appreciated the grind mentality as much as the next millennial, but he also felt it was important to find time for himself during the week. Besides, he had a tee time at the Peachtree Golf Club in the morning.

Three hours on the links is just what I need, he told himself as he turned off the lights to his office.

As Friday slowly turned into Saturday, though, he found himself becoming more and more anxious at the prospect of having to speak before the senior executives of his company.

He pulled into the parking lot of the golf course Saturday morning and began to unload his clubs, his thoughts drifting back to a piece of wisdom he heard from Coach Valvano that he had tucked away in his brain.

The relationship between hard work and success is not direct, he reminded himself. *It's not if you work hard, you'll be successful. It's if you don't work hard, you've got no shot.*[1]

Joey had lived his life up to that point believing that if you work hard, you will be successful, but the more he thought about it, the more he realized that Coach Valvano was right.

Hard work didn't guarantee success at all.

In fact, he could think of plenty of people who put in the hours at their jobs only to be laid off or never really ascend the corporate ladder.

I guess it comes down to how you define success. Still, hard work is important, he told himself. His work ethic was the reason he had gotten this far in his career.

He had put in the long hours, stayed late when everyone else

---

1. Holladay, Daniel. "Jimmy V-Cutting Down the Nets." Online video clip. Youtube. 14 Mar 2017.

had gone home, and come in on the weekends when there was no one around but the custodial staff.

Heck, I'm going to be doing that again this weekend, he thought.

His team had been putting in the work too. No one was ducking out early. They were all there, and they were finally all engaged. It seemed unfair to think that his team was working this hard with nothing to show for it.

Why put in the work at all? he thought briefly as he loaded his clubs into the cart and headed to the first tee. *If we're just going to get raked over the coals for not solving the problem, why should we give our best effort in the first place?*

His cynical sentiment was eerily familiar to the tone used by Sam the first time he assembled the team together.

Joey knew better than to actually believe that hard work wasn't necessary. He valued effort more than most, and he had made up his mind that he would be committed and embody the standards and values representing what he wanted the team to stand for.

Still, he knew it wouldn't be easy on Monday morning when he stood there with nothing to show for the labors of his team.

He walked up to the first hole and placed a golf ball on a tee. He pulled out his driver from his bag, took a couple of practice swings, and in one swift motion tried to erase all the frustrations of feeling that he was on the right path, doing things the right way, but none of that would matter.

The golf ball sailed into the air, picking up speed as it bounded down the right side of the fairway before coming to a stop 150 yards out from the green.

One shot on the golf course wasn't going to be enough to rid the young leader of all his concerns, but it sure felt good to rip one right down the middle.

He hopped in the golf cart and took off toward his ball, still admiring his tee shot and trying to put the upcoming meeting out of his mind.

He pulled a seven iron out of the bag, sizing up his second shot before standing over the ball and preparing to try and take some more frustration out on the little white dimpled sphere.

As he put the club head behind the ball and commenced his backswing, he heard a shout from the next hole over.

"FORE!" yelled a man to his right, his ball flying through the trees between them and heading right for Joey.

The young leader covered his head and ducked, bracing for impact as the ball hit several tree limbs before rolling through and stopping a few yards from where he stood.

The man began to drive over to where Joey was standing, apologizing from a long distance away.

As he came into focus, Joey couldn't believe his eyes.

It was Marcus.

The old man clearly wasn't as good at golf as he was at giving advice.

"Joey! Funny running into you here!" Marcus exclaimed as he pulled up next to his young protégé.

"I was going to say the same thing," the young leader responded, realizing fairly quickly that these moments could no longer be considered pure coincidence.

"It's as if you know every time I have a negative thought. Let me guess, another perk of the job!"

"You could say that!" Marcus said. "Lucky for you, I haven't been able to get rid of this slice in my swing."

Joey explained to Marcus what had taken place over the rest of his week. He told him about the trip to Robins Air Force Base and the newfound level of motivation and commitment his team seemed to be displaying. He explained how hard they had been working and how he felt they were close to a real breakthrough.

And then Joey told Marcus about the meeting on Monday, how he was going to have to answer for the team's lack of success, and how he was questioning himself once again, this time wondering if all the hard work was even worth it.

Marcus motioned to the next group of golfers behind them to play through as he took in what Joey was saying.

"So, let me get this straight," he asked the young businessman. "Even though you understand the relationship between hard work and success, you are still questioning the necessity of effort?"

"It's not that I'm questioning working hard. I understand that you can't be successful without it. I've seen that in my own life; I believe in working hard. But realizing that hard work doesn't guarantee success in your endeavors makes it hard to feel like all the effort is worth it if in the end you just come up short."

"That's a very honest admission, and I appreciate your willingness to share your doubts," Marcus responded. "But...it's not about the success. The success is just a byproduct of the effort, and we don't put forth the effort simply to see the success. We put forth the effort because it's all part of the process of becoming who we want to be, of realizing our best selves, of achieving that *eudaimonic* flourishing in our lives.

"Results matter in our world and I understand that. But if you become a person of great effort, and the reason you are focused on putting forth great effort is because you know it's the only way to realize true excellence in your own life and, in turn, help those around you realize true excellence in their lives, the results will take care of themselves."

As Joey was trying to process Marcus' words, another group of golfers approached, interrupting his focus.

"I could keep going on for a while on this one, but we can't hold up everyone else on the golf course," Marcus exclaimed. He reached into his pocket and pulled out a coin. "Here, let me show you what I mean instead!"

Joey got a quick glimpse at the coin. He saw a pair of boxing gloves above the word παιδεία.

Even as he got used to seeing the coins, he was still mesmerized by the intricacies found on each one.

Marcus gave the coin a toss, the bright flash of light fading quickly as Joey suddenly found himself seated in a dimly lit auditorium. He was surrounded by a bunch of fancily clad men who seemed to be waiting anxiously to hear remarks from someone on the stage in front of them.

Joey looked around, trying to find some indication of where he was, but there was nothing of importance that would signify their location.

The room was packed. There was a buzz of excitement in the air as they waited for the speech to begin.

He guessed they had arrived in the early twentieth century. This assumption was based solely on the attire of the men in the room, all of them were decked out in three-piece suits with big bowler hats. It felt like an elite club, a who's who of businessmen and gentlemen of high society.

"1899. Chicago. The Hamilton Club," Marcus declared, answering every question Joey had as succinctly as possible. Pointing toward the stage, he indicated to Joey that his short responses were due to the fact that the speaker was now being introduced.

As the gentleman walked toward the center of the stage, Joey didn't need to hear the introduction. The man's distinct comb-over, spectacles, and bushy mustache left no doubt to his identity. He looked like every picture of Theodore Roosevelt Joey had ever seen.

Joey thought how each of these journeys pointed out how little he actually remembered from U.S. history class.

He knew TR's image was on Mount Rushmore, he was considered one of the greatest presidents in history, he commanded the Rough Riders in the Spanish-American War, and he was an advocate for establishing the National Parks system. That was all Joey could remember, though, and his limited knowledge did little to explain why he was here.

Teddy Roosevelt walked to the stage and began to speak.

Joey slid forward in his chair, preparing to soak in every word. The chance to hear from another of America's great presidents in person was an opportunity he would not take for granted.

From the first words he uttered, the reason Marcus had brought him here became distinctly clear.

"I wish to preach, not the doctrine of ignoble ease, but the doctrine of the strenuous life. The life of toil and effort, of labor and strife; to preach that highest form of success which comes, not to the man who desires mere easy peace, but to the man who does not shrink from danger, from hardship or from bitter toil, and who out of these wins the splendid ultimate triumph."[2]

The future President continued, the words resounding throughout the auditorium as he spoke.

"We do not admire the man of timid peace. We admire the man who embodies victorious effort; the man who never wrongs his neighbor, who is prompt to help a friend, but who has those virile qualities necessary to win in the stern strife of actual life. It is hard to fail, but it is worse never to have tried to succeed."[3]

Joey looked at Marcus with a glance that indicated the exactness with which the old man had diagnosed his current struggle.

"Far better it is to dare mighty things, to win glorious tri-

2. Roosevelt, Theodore. "The Strenuous Life."
http://voicesofdemocracy.umd.edu/roosevelt-strenuous-life-1899-speech-text/.
Accessed 5 Apr 2018.
3. Ibid.

umphs, even though checkered by failure, than to take rank with those poor spirits who neither enjoy much nor suffer much, because they live in the gray twilight that knows not victory nor defeat."[4]

The Governor of New York was speaking right to the young man, his words piercing Joey's soul as he brought home his message with fervor and intensity, his fist shaking as he solidified each point.

"We have a given problem to solve. If we undertake the solution, there is, of course, always danger that we may not solve it, but to refuse to undertake the solution simply renders it certain that we cannot possibly solve it."[5]

This was exactly what Joey needed to hear. He knew deep down that in order to lead, in order to be someone worth following, he needed to be a man unafraid of taking on the hard things of life, undaunted by the problems at hand. Deciding not to act, not to put forth the effort, not to do the hard work, meant there would be no chance to solve the problem facing his team.

Teddy Roosevelt continued. "The work must be done; we cannot escape our responsibility; and if we are worth our salt, we shall be glad of the chance to do the work."[6]

"Glad to do the work," Joey repeated to himself. "It's not just about the necessity of the work itself."

Roosevelt was suggesting that above the essentialness of work to achieve greatness was a pleasure that could be taken from even being given the opportunity to do the work in the first place.

"But to do this work, keep ever in mind that we must show in a very high degree the qualities of courage, of honesty, and of good judgment."[7]

Now he's suggesting that it wasn't just doing the work; it was how

---

4. Ibid.
5. Ibid.
6. Ibid.
7. Ibid.

you did the work, Joey thought, taking each word to heart. *It's not just doing it, but doing it the right way.*

Marcus could see the young man deciphering the lessons for himself. He looked over and nodded in agreement as the leader in the young man continued to grow.

"Let us therefore boldly face the life of strife, resolute to do our duty well and manfully; resolute to uphold righteousness by deed and by word; resolute to be both honest and brave, to serve high ideals. Above all, let us shrink from no strife, moral or physical, within or without the nation, provided we are certain that the strife is justified, for it is only through strife, through hard and dangerous endeavor, that we shall ultimately win the goal of true national greatness."[8]

Marcus flipped the coin again as the future twenty-sixth president of the United States finished his remarks.

They emerged back on the first fairway, the same group of golfers passing them by as Joey stood back over his ball. Time had stood still, the two of them transported back to the exact moment they left.

"Alright, that was the perfect speech for me to hear right now. It was as though you knew exactly what I needed in order to keep moving forward."

"Delivering what is needed to those who need it when they need it, am I right?" Marcus replied.

"Exactly!" Joey said, finding humor in the reference.

"So, what was it specifically that was so impactful?" Marcus asked.

"When he talked about the man who embraces the strenuous life, who embodies great effort, who isn't afraid to fail because they would rather fail than not try at all, that really struck me. When he mentioned that if we refuse to undertake the solution then we certainly can't solve it. That we should be glad to do the

---

8. Ibid.

work, to do the hard things, and that we should do it all by pursuing those efforts in the right way. Those things all hit home.

"If I'm not prepared to put forth the effort, if I'm not the kind of leader who establishes a standard of seeking excellence through the difficult challenges, then how can I possibly expect the team to do the same? I've always been a person who was willing to outwork anyone. That's how I was raised. And this reminded me of why the work is important to begin with."

"Those are all fantastic observations. You are starting to discern many parts of what it really means to lead. You know, you brought up the word *excellence*. The Greeks used the word *arete* to mean that which is always excellent. It was synonymous with the word *virtue*. It represented the highest achievement of one's potential. The pursuit of that level of excellence in everything you do requires great effort. Like I said before, though, it's not about effort for the sake of achieving results.

"It's about putting forth the effort and living the strenuous life because that is part of seeking your highest potential, of living your own life of *arete* in everything you do. When you understand how to pursue your own highest level of excellence, then and only then, can you help others seek excellence in their own lives. And, that, my friend, is what this whole thing is all about."

"So, it *is* about working harder than everyone else, then?"

"No. It's not just about the effort. Being busy isn't synonymous with real work. Just being there to show everyone you are there doesn't mean you are actually pursuing the strenuous life. The strenuous life is about never shying away from the difficult things. It means that you aren't afraid to pursue what seems impossible, to put yourself in the arena, to get bloodied, to fail, to exhaust yourself in a worthy cause, and to dare greatly. You should be willing to do what it takes if you have determined that the cause is worthy, but as you pointed out, how you are spending your energy and considering why you are pursuing a life of great effort in the first place are just as important.

"Theodore Roosevelt tried to live the strenuous life because he realized as a young boy that he was going to have to do so in order to get by. He battled severe asthma as a child, which led him to begin bodybuilding as a way of strengthening himself and fighting the weaknesses of his body. After being bullied and beaten on a train one day, he realized even that wasn't enough. If he wanted to succeed physically, he was going to have to join what he called 'the fellowship of the doers.'[9] He doubled his efforts. He started boxing. He put his body through an intense physical regimen that he maintained throughout his life.

"He pushed himself mentally as well, consuming books at a rapid pace, becoming an amateur taxidermist, and writing one of the greatest accounts of the War of 1812, among other pursuits. Though he came from a family of great wealth and prosperity, he sought a life free of idleness of any kind.

"Even as he pursued excellence vigorously both physically and mentally, it was the words his father gave him before he left for Harvard that rang true for Teddy his entire life: 'Take care of your morals first.'[10] That's why he sought the strenuous life. He believed that who he was, and who he was becoming, was dependent on keeping his values properly aligned with his actions, and for him, that meant seeking out difficult things.

"It's how he came to be a cowboy in the Dakotas, lead the Rough Riders in Cuba, win a Nobel Peace Prize for bringing an end to the Russo-Japanese War, and become the youngest president in United States history.

"Here's the kicker though," Marcus said, as another group of golfers caught up to them. "Teddy Roosevelt wasn't just a man with a tireless work ethic. He was also a man of incredible discipline. It was said that 'Iron self-discipline [became] a habit with him.'[11]

---

9. Morris, Edmund. *The Rise of Theodore Roosevelt*. New York: Coward, McCann & Geoghegan, 1979. Page 35.

10. Ibid, Page 73.

11. Ibid, Page 64.

"The actual amount of time that he spent at his desk working each day was actually relatively small, but his concentration and his ability to focus was so intense that he could do more in a quarter of the time than most of his colleagues could with their entire day.[12] So you see, it's not about working for the sake of working. It's about habituating a life of iron self-discipline in the same vein as TR.

"Roosevelt was prepared for each timely opportunity in his life because he understood the importance of self-discipline. He knew what was important to him, and he pursued those things. He wasn't distracted with things that didn't matter. This is the culmination of the strenuous life that we must pursue. We must pursue the worthy causes and do so with a disciplined effort."

"I guess I've never really thought that much about what discipline really means," Joey said, looking ahead toward the first green.

"Discipline is doing the right thing at the right time in the right way for the right reasons," the old man replied. "Discipline creates efficiency in how you live your life. It's like that seven iron you are holding there," Marcus said, taking the club out of Joey's hands. "You know why I'm a terrible golfer?"

"I don't know. Because you don't play enough to be good?" Joey responded.

"No. I play golf every week. I love the game of golf. I would say I put a lot of effort into playing golf, actually. But I'm not any good because I don't do the right things in the right way at the right time that are necessary to become great at golf. I just come out here and swing away, trying to drive the ball as far as possible. I put in the work, so to speak, but there is no discipline in how I pursue the work."

"So, practice makes perfect, is that what you're saying?" Joey said.

---

12. Ibid, Page 64.

"Practice doesn't make perfect, son. Practice makes *permanent*. I can't get rid of that slice that almost took your head off because I've made a bad habit permanent. Deliberate practice makes perfect. If I came out and actually worked on my short game, actually focused on hitting this seven iron from 150 yards out, actually spent my time doing the little things that lead to excellence as a golfer, maybe I would become a great golfer someday.

"It's all about creating proper moral habits, and those habits come directly from your ability to live a life of self-discipline, to pursue *arete* in everything you do. Deliberate practice is about discovering the things that you need to work on, the things that will get you where you want to go, the things that are worthy of your time, and pursuing those things consistently, over and over again, with an enthusiasm and effort that matches their worth, until you master those things. That's pursuing the common things in life in an uncommon way.

"That's how you learn to live a life full of *arete*, a life that will command the attention of the world—not because of the great accomplishments or successes you have, but because you have learned what it means to be excellent and have passed that on to others.

"That's what **LDL** is all about."

Joey took his club back from Marcus and stood once again over his ball. He thought about what he had seen, about how his view of work and effort had shifted, and about what Marcus had just said about the importance of discipline in the pursuit of excellence in his life. He reared the club back behind him and gave a fluid swing, striking the ball perfectly and watching as it sailed ahead, landing softly on the green, mere feet from the pin.

"That was deliberate all right!" he exclaimed, turning back toward Marcus, but he was gone.

Man, I thought we were past the disappearing act. Joey laughed to himself as he hopped in the cart and continued his relaxing day on the links.

The young leader spent the rest of the afternoon thinking hard about what his own life would look like if he approached it the way President Roosevelt had suggested.

He really believed that a life of great effort was important to becoming his best version of himself, but it was what Marcus shared about self-discipline that really paved the way for him to move forward.

As a former athlete, Joey understood discipline. He knew how much effort had to go into the little things to create the opportunity for the big things. He knew that the work spent alone in the gym seen by no one was what allowed someone to shine under the bright lights. He understood the importance of forming proper habits, but it was never something he considered important to who he was as a leader. He never thought forming "moral" habits could be accomplished in the same way.

Perhaps if he could really embody self-discipline in every area of his life, and consistently align his actions with the values he had identified as most important just weeks earlier, he could discover what *arete* truly meant.

Joey arrived at work Sunday afternoon, ready to attack his upcoming presentation with the proper effort and enthusiasm.

When he finally made it up the elevator to the twenty-third floor, he was shocked at what he saw. Several members of his team were there, toiling away, preparing for the presentation that he was responsible for giving the next morning.

Not everyone had made it in, but Joey never expected any of them to be there. He had made that very clear in his email the night before.

The fact that Jill, Cathy, Ron, Liz, and Jenny had shown up left him speechless.

He walked over to Jill, who was frantically trying to put the financials together for him to brief. He asked her why they had decided to come to help him get ready.

"Because," she said, "we know you would have done the same for us!"

Perhaps he still had a lot left to learn, but at that moment, Joey received all the confirmation he could possibly want that he was well on his way to becoming the type of leader his team needed.

He quickly got to work, focusing his efforts on what was important to prepare himself and the team for the worthy cause in front of them.

CHAPTER 7
Ἁμαρτία
FAILURE

"Failure isn't fatal, but failure to change might be."

—JOHN WOODEN

J OEY STOOD OUTSIDE the boardroom waiting to be summoned in for his presentation.

It had been a few years since he had felt this level of pressure.
He had butterflies in his stomach, the nerves reminiscent of all
those times right before big games sitting in the locker room in
anticipation of what was to come, replaying in his mind everything he could remember from film study and practice before
going to battle with his teammates.

He knew there would be a level of dissatisfaction at his team's
lack of results thus far. He had spent a large portion of the day
before preparing himself for that line of questioning. In his mind,
it was inevitable at this juncture, but he fully believed in where
they were headed, the standards they were collectively buying
into, and their overall commitment to the vision.

Maybe it had taken them longer to get to this point than the
board would have liked, but if he could just convince them that
they were on the verge of a big breakthrough and that they would
be able to do so without sacrificing the quality of the products
they were creating, surely they would tell him to press ahead.

He even took the time to draw up his team's bridge, capturing the purpose, vision, dreams, goals, and standards he had implemented to get them to this point.

He was nervous, but his belief in himself and his team was at an all-time high. He was committed like never before, and he had worked hard to put selfish thoughts out of his mind and focus on the team and what he could do to bring them up to their highest potential. He felt as though he finally understood how to harness self-motivation to help inspire his team to their own version of a life of excellence.

He was ready with an outline of what was most important, what was worthy of his team's time, and how a disciplined pursuit of those things coupled with the proper deliberate practice would form in them the right habits and propel them forward at an even faster pace.

He walked into the boardroom confident in himself and his team. Things weren't perfect, but he felt more than ever that he was the right man for the job. Not only were they going to be able to solve this problem, but the way they were going to do it would set the foundation for a culture of sustained success that would spread throughout the various departments of the company.

As optimistic as he was, however, the board had made up its own mind about how the meeting was going to go before he ever entered the room.

From the moment he walked in, they made it clear that they only cared about why his team had failed to meet their quarterly projections and how they had been unable to come up with a solution after being together for nearly two months.

Everything Joey did to try and reassure them that they were on the brink of success fell on deaf ears. They raked him across the coals for his lack of productivity, questioned his approach to managing his team, and chastised him over his ability to actually lead.

Also invited to the meeting was Bill, the VP of Manufacturing, and he had done everything in his power to deflect blame Joey's way, call him out for the losses in revenue, question his decision-making ability, and paint him as inflexible and unwilling to listen to any ideas that emerged from his team if it meant lowering the quality of the parts temporarily.

Joey couldn't believe that the other members of the board found Bill's attacks acceptable. How could they put stock prices and revenue above the quality of the products they were delivering, especially when those products would be used by the country's brave service members?

Greg, the company's COO, seemed to be the only person in attendance willing to hear out the young leader. He brushed aside the comments from Bill and the other members of the board. He was genuinely intrigued at Joey's conviction that the best was yet to come.

He appreciated the bridge, the deliberateness with which Joey approached his role and the vision he had cast for his team, and though he too was concerned with the lack of results, he empathized with the difficult situation Joey was facing.

If not for him, Joey was certain he would have been relieved of his temporary leadership role and replaced by someone else. Or perhaps the team would have simply been disbanded altogether.

Nevertheless, Greg stepped in and worked out a compromise with the rest of his executive team. Joey would be granted two more weeks to come up with a solution and then report back to the board with his proposed plan moving forward.

Joey felt relieved that as badly as that had gone, he still had the opportunity to lead his team for a few more weeks. He wasn't kidding himself, though. A two-week extension was better than the alternative, but he knew it would add even more pressure to the team.

He had heard rumors that it was Greg who nominated him for the position to begin with, and he was beginning to wonder what the company's executive saw in him in the first place. If the last hour was any indication, the COO might be the only person left who still believed in his potential.

Though he was appreciative of Greg's willingness to stick his neck out for him, Joey also couldn't help but feel like a complete failure as a leader.

Marcus had continued to preach patience, telling him that the journey he was on as a leader was a lifelong one, a continuous learning experience that he couldn't rush, but right now he was frustrated with himself. He wasn't sure how he was going to break the news to the team, or what he could say to dampen their anxiety.

He tried to fall back on the things he had learned over the last few weeks. He thought back to Coach Swinney, the interim head coach with no previous experience in the role who had earned the full-time job in the end.

Maybe, just maybe, this would work out for him in the same way too.

Everyone else had trickled out of the meeting, returning to their spacious offices on the twenty-fifth floor.

Joey stayed behind, pacing back and forth. He knew his team was anxious to hear the outcome, and he wanted to be the one to deliver the news to them before any rumors started swirling around two stories below.

He continued to walk across the room, looking down at the beautiful hardwoods below. Sinking his hands in his pockets, he released himself from the professional environment of the board meeting and back to a much more casual feeling as he pondered the best delivery approach.

Inside his pocket he felt an object that had not been there when he entered the room. It didn't take a rocket scientist to figure out what it was or who had somehow found a way to slip it in.

He wasn't sure how Marcus possibly could have put a coin in his pocket, since he hadn't seen his mentor since the golf outing on Friday, and this was a brand new pair of pants that he had broken out specifically for the occasion of addressing the board, but at this point, who was he to question the tactics of the old man? Neither time nor space seemed to be a factor for what he could conjure up, but accurately predicting the future and making something appear out of thin air seemed excessively far-fetched, even to Joey.

The only word he could think of at this point was *magic*. What else could this be?

He pulled out the coin and saw the familiar **LDL** logo. He turned the coin over, revealing an old hat that looked more like something that would accompany a kid's Halloween costume than an ancient relic, with the word Αμαρτία inscribed below.

There was no letter this time warning him of impending danger or any reason he shouldn't take this trip on his own.

He knew that time would stand still while he was on his journey, so he rationalized that he would still be able to break the news to his team before anyone else would have a chance to get to them first. Joey took a deep breath and tossed the coin in the air, the customary blinding light becoming routine enough that he timed the closing of his eyes to avoid exposure.

There wasn't much for him to discern this time around. He was in the middle of a beautiful park, surrounded by elegant, columned brick buildings, with thousands of chairs laid out perfectly throughout the lawn, all accompanied by onlookers who were decked out in academic regalia.

Joey wasn't sure of the location, but it was evident that he was at a commencement ceremony for an institution of higher learning.

"Marcus sure is a sucker for a good speech," he told himself, leaning against one of the many trees to listen to the speaker deliver their prepared remarks.

He thought back to his own graduation from business school. He couldn't even remember who the speaker was that day or what they said, but he remembered feeling prepared at that moment to take on anything. He had a top degree in hand, the world was at his fingertips, and he had secured a brand-new job that would send him to downtown Atlanta to work for one of the top companies in the region.

Seems like a lifetime ago now! he thought. *If twenty-four-year-old me could see the disaster I just experienced, I'm pretty sure he wouldn't be quite so eager to get away from the comforts of college and out into real life.*

The speaker walked forward to the podium, her quaint floral-themed dress fluttering in the breeze as she began to address those in attendance.

Her first words cemented their location.

She thanked the president, board, faculty, parents, and graduates of Harvard University for giving her the opportunity to speak with them on this momentous day.[1]

The next few seconds confirmed her identity.

She mentioned that all she needed to do to get past the fear of delivering her thoughts was to close her eyes and pretend that all the Crimson banners surrounding her meant that she was at the "world's largest Gryffindor reunion."[2]

This was J.K. Rowling, author of the world-renowned and immensely popular Harry Potter series.

Joey immediately perked up at the literary reference, the child in him delighted at the discovery that the speaker was someone he had never met but felt deeply connected to.

---

1. Rowling, J.K. "The Fringe Benefits of Failure, and the Importance of Imagination." *https://news.harvard.edu/gazette/story/2008/06/text-of-j-k-rowling-speech/.* Accessed 3 May 2018.
2. Ibid.

He had devoured her books as a kid. Unable to put them down, he spent hours and days at a time lost in his own imagination and following Harry, Ron Weasley, and Hermione Granger throughout their years at the Hogwarts School of Witchcraft and Wizardry as they defended the wizarding world against Voldemort and his Death Eaters, all while traveling on their own adolescent journeys of self-discovery.

For a brief moment, it didn't matter what Rowling was going to say. Joey was simply ecstatic that he would get the opportunity to hear from his all-time favorite author. Once she began to talk, though, the kid in him gave way to the present, bringing him back to his current situation. Joey found himself mesmerized by her spoken words in the same way he had been by those she had written for the world over the last decade.

This wasn't a boilerplate speech about chasing your dreams and finding happiness, as so many graduation remarks tend to be. No, from the very outset, Rowling made it clear that she intended to speak to them not strictly about all the successes they would find in life, but about the moments of struggle that would provide each of them with the opportunity to learn the "benefits of failure."[3]

She admitted that this could be construed as a "paradoxical choice," given the occasion which they found themselves celebrating, but when she really thought about what she would want her twenty-one-year-old self to know, nothing seemed more important than understanding what failure really is and what it can do.[4]

Rowling talked about how all she ever really wanted to do was write novels, but her parents wanted her to find a "vocational degree" that would provide a steady income. Her parents had been poor, and she had experienced poverty in her own adult life, so she couldn't blame them for wanting her to avoid that circumstance. As she said, "It is not an ennobling experience."[5]

---

3. Ibid.
4. Ibid.

But far beyond her concern about disappointing her parents was the fear of failure that overcame her at a young age. Up to that point for her, success had been defined by scores on tests and examinations, and she admitted that even though the students she was addressing probably had experienced some level of failure in their lives, the fact that they were graduating from Harvard would suggest that they are "not very well-acquainted with [it]."[6]

Joey could relate. For all intents and purposes, he had experienced little failure in his life. Sure, he had lost some big games on the basketball court, and he had struggled with a few tests every now and then, and everything had not been perfect at his job from day one, but on the whole, he had realized what he set out to achieve. A Division One scholarship, a top MBA, on the cusp of a corner office at such a young age—there hadn't been much that had gone wrong for him.

Yet, just like Rowling, he was often crippled by a fear of failure, and he wasn't sure why. When he thought of the words he had heard just a few days ago from Theodore Roosevelt about the strenuous life, about doing the hard things, it all sounded wonderful—except for the possibility that, in trying, he might fall short in achieving his dreams.

He wasn't afraid of the work it would take, or of learning to live a complete life of discipline, but he was afraid of not being good enough to lead his team and of being a failure in their eyes.

"By any conventional measure, a mere seven years after my graduation day, I had failed on an epic scale."[7]

Rowling's words snapped Joey back to the moment at hand. He was hearing from someone who, at almost the same age he was now, had been divorced, jobless, a single parent, and "as poor as it is possible to be in modern Britain without being homeless."[8]

---

5. Ibid.
6. Ibid.
7. Ibid.
8. Ibid.

Yet it was at that point, when all around her seemed to be falling apart, that she had her breakthrough, completing the manuscript for the first Harry Potter novel in coffee shops around Edinburgh and transcribing the generational work on an old typewriter she had purchased with what little money she had.

Her success was just on the horizon, and though she couldn't see it then, it was failure that allowed that moment to come to fruition.

She admitted that there wasn't much fun about failure or that period of her life. She couldn't always see the light at the end of the tunnel or how far that tunnel even extended at times, but it was through the darkest period of her life that she found true meaning.

"I stopped pretending to myself that I was anything other than what I was and began to direct all my energy into finishing the only work that mattered to me."[9]

She spoke about authenticity and purpose, things Marcus had harped on from day one.

"I was set free because my greatest fear had been realized, and I was still alive, and I still had a daughter whom I adored, and I had an old typewriter and a big idea. And so rock bottom became the solid foundation on which I rebuilt my life."[10]

She shared how she had found freedom in failure and her deepest fear coming true. She had emerged from the other side still there, ready to fight for her purpose and big idea about the "boy who lived."

Rowling then spoke of the inevitability of failure—that is, unless you are too timid to even try, in which case you might as well have not lived at all and "you fail by default."[11]

She summarized the thoughts Joey had heard expressed so succinctly by Teddy Roosevelt just a few days prior. Spend yourself in

---

9. Ibid.
10. Ibid.
11. Ibid.

a worthy cause, and if you fail, at least "fail while daring greatly, so that [your] place shall never be with those cold and timid souls who know neither victory or defeat."[12]

That's what Joey wanted.

He wanted to be in the arena. He wanted the opportunity to lead this team, help them all reach their potential, find in themselves a life of excellence, and become the best versions of themselves each and every day. Joey wanted to dare greatly, even if failure, as he had just experienced, would be inevitable along the way.

Rowling finished her points by focusing on what she learned about herself through failure. She shared how she emerged wiser and stronger from her setbacks, how she became more aware of herself and what she was capable of enduring through adversity, and how, even though it was "painfully won, it has been worth more than any qualification ever earned."[13]

As she moved on to her next topic, Joey sensed that he had heard what Marcus intended for him. Here was someone he admired who had experienced more failure than he could imagine and ended up on the other side of it one of the most successful women in the world.

Perhaps his little setback wasn't so bad after all. Even more importantly, maybe it could help him in ways he hadn't considered.

The coin went sailing back up in the air, and Joey found himself standing in the conference room once again.

"There he is!" he heard Marcus bellow.

Confused at how the old man could possibly be waiting for him if no time had passed since he left, Joey blurted out, "How did you even get in here?"

---

12. Roosevelt, Theodore. "Citizenship in a Republic." *http://www.theodore-roosevelt.com/trsorbonnespeech.html*. Accessed 3 May 2018.

13. Rowling, J.K. "The Fringe Benefits of Failure, and the Importance of Imagination." *https://news.harvard.edu/gazette/story/2008/06/text-of-j-k-rowling-speech/*. Accessed 3 May 2018.

But before Marcus could respond, Joey said, "Never mind. It doesn't matter. I do have to say, though, that once again, you've outdone yourself, my friend. You sent me to the perfect moment in time for the perfect lesson. Another speech that was spot on!"

Marcus looked perplexed. "I didn't send you anywhere. I just came by to see how the meeting went."

"Well then, who put this in my pocket?" Joey said, equally puzzled about what had taken place. He pulled the coin out and showed it to the old man.

"Ah, that's a good one," Marcus declared as he twirled the coin between his fingers. "Rowling. Harvard. The failure speech. I'm guessing the meeting didn't go so hot then?"

"No, it was terrible. From the start they never even gave me a chance. And if it wasn't for our COO, I don't think I would still be leading my team. I've got two weeks to come up with a solution and implement it. Two weeks to make or break my career here."

"That's great! Two more weeks to pour into the lives of everyone you are in charge of leading."

"More like two weeks to find a way to go from one end of the spectrum to the other, from failure to success."

Marcus pursed his lips. "So you believe that the opposite of success is failure then?"

"Yeah, of course. I'm pretty sure Merriam-Webster would agree with me too," Joey replied.

"How we think about failure will ultimately determine how we approach it, how we respond to it, what we do with it, and what it does to us," Marcus declared. "It doesn't matter what the dictionary or the thesaurus says; it only matters how *you* define success and failure and how *you* perceive their relationship."

Pausing a moment to let that sink in, Marcus continued. "I know you know who John Wooden is."

"Of course. I couldn't have played college basketball and not known about arguably the greatest man that ever coached the sport. Ten National Championships in twelve seasons, including seven in a row. He's an absolute legend!"

"Then you know about his pyramid of success, right?"

"Yeah, I've seen it before. It detailed his beliefs about what it took to build competitive greatness in any endeavor."

"Correct. Well, we at **LDL** have our own pyramid, and it's something I hope to show you one day soon, but now is not the time. I bring it up, though, because Wooden defined success as 'peace of mind which is a direct result of self-satisfaction in knowing you made the effort to become the best of which you are capable.'[14]

"If success is about consistently working to become the best version of yourself, then we at **LDL** believe that as a leader, success is about consistently working to help those you are entrusted with leading become the best versions of themselves. Our organization's purpose is very literal, after all. We are Leaders Developing Leaders. If that's what you are striving for, then success isn't based on wins, losses, or P&L statements. Those things will forever keep failure and success as opposites in your mind, and if you let them, they will take away from what really matters.

"That's not to say that those things aren't important, but they should serve to enhance the need for your purpose, vision, standards, commitment, belief, and a disciplined pursuit of excellence, not define what makes you a successful organization. Through habituating those things in your life, you come to realize that your definition of success is about so much more, and failure, which as J.K. Rowling pointed out is inevitable, is not the opposite of success at all. Failure, my friend, is the partner of success."

"The partner? So I'm supposed to be OK with failure then?"

"Absolutely not! No one is saying that you should simply accept failure—quite the opposite actually. All the things we've talked about—striving for *arete*, finding your own level of *eudai-*

---

14. Wooden, John. "Pyramid of Success." *http://www.coachwooden.com/pyramid-of-success.* Accessed 18 May 2018.

monia—they all push you toward sustained excellence in life. But they also change your attitude toward failure.

"There are only three certainties in life: death, taxes, and failure. Failure is going to happen, and once you understand that fact and no longer see it as the polar opposite of what you are trying to achieve, suddenly the setbacks and shortcomings become catalysts for accelerated growth through proper reflection as opposed to merely a mechanism for disbelief and uncertainty. When that happens, the river raging in the gap below your bridge becomes a little less scary.

"If you approach failure as the partner to success, then failure reinforces your purpose, reaffirms the need for proper standards, enhances your commitment, challenges your belief level, and keeps you focused on what really matters. And as a leader, it changes how you see and respond to your team and their failures as well.

"All leaders are teachers, and success by itself is a pretty lousy teacher. Failure, when it's no longer the enemy, when it's no longer crippling your team out of fear of falling short, becomes a teachable moment, and your response to failure begins to change. Failure becomes something you can use to call people up to where you know they can be, even though they may still be uncertain of their own potential."

"So, I'm supposed to just let my team fail?" Joey exclaimed, still uncertain of what Marcus was really saying.

"Don't get it confused. You hold your team accountable to your standards. If you don't hold them accountable to your standards, you are simply telling them one of two things. You are either telling them, 'I don't think you are good enough to meet our standards in the first place,' or 'I don't care enough about you to hold you to our standards.'

"Those standards are your code. They keep the vision from collapsing into the river of doubt below. But falling short in something isn't the same as not upholding the standard. The standard is about who we are, what we represent, how we approach the challenges that are presented to us. It's not about winning every game, closing the deal with every client, or meeting every production goal.

"You hold people accountable to the standard because those standards are rooted in your collective values. You know that those collective values represent who you want to be as a team, and that together, they will take the team to its own collective level of *arete*." Marcus paused for a moment and then went on. "Do you know what an expansion joint is?"

"No, I don't believe so," Joey replied.

"Expansion joints give bridges 'breathing room.' They allow the concrete to expand and contract without cracking. Visions built by leaders without expansion joints eventually crack under pressure. Leaders who are terrified of allowing room for error, of what could happen if someone saw their failures or their team's struggles, operate out of fear, working to eliminate any and all mistakes and keeping the ones that do occur from ever seeing the light of day. They keep their concrete filled to capacity throughout their bridge. Eventually the vision cracks under the weight of a misapplied attempt at perfection. Failure serves as the expansion joint in your bridge.

"Respond to failure in a way that allows room for growth, that encourages reflection, that empowers people to become better. *Perfection* isn't the standard; *best* is the standard. Best allows for failure because failure is an essential component of keeping the vision intact and ultimately making it a reality.

"If you properly orient your attitude towards failure, then your response to failure as a leader will change. When that happens, failure is no longer removed from the equation or avoided at all costs, but rather is a component of the overall code you have built and included in seeing those purpose inspired dreams come true."

"I certainly have never thought of failure that way," Joey said. "It's always been something I've tried to eliminate, not something I've used to enhance who I'm becoming. I think we are going to need a few expansion joints in the bridge over the next two weeks, that's for sure. We certainly added one today without even knowing it was coming. I still don't understand, though— how did that coin get in my pocket?"

"Well, only an **LDL** member would have access to this coin. Either that, or I've been working really hard on my levitation skills," Marcus said, flicking his wrist to imitate the motion of a wand.

Joey chuckled and put the curious conundrum out of his mind. It was time to get back to his team and break the news before they heard it secondhand.

"Well, as always, thank you for everything," the young leader said, truly appreciative of Marcus' willingness to share so much with him. "Time to head down two floors and practice my response to failure, and make sure the team knows just what I think of the board's irresponsible decision and willingness to throw us all under the bus."

CHAPTER 8

Ιδιοκτησία
OWNERSHIP

*"A sense of ownership is the most powerful weapon a team
or organization can have."*

—Pat Summitt

JOEY BARELY HAD time to turn around. He hadn't even taken
a step toward the door before he heard Marcus calling out to
him.

"Hey, hold up! You aren't really about to go tell your team that
are you?"

"Absolutely! I'm going to let them know that I disagree
strongly with the decision that has been made. Two weeks isn't
enough time to figure this out, and the way I, I mean the way
we, are being treated by Bill and some of the members of the
board isn't fair. It was Bill's insistence about shifting to automation before we were certain of the production outcome that put
us in this predicament in the first place. And now he is trying to
pin all the blame on me for everything."

"Oh boy," Marcus declared softly. "I don't think you understand the negative impact of what you are about to do, son. Nor-
mally I'd be more than happy to let you figure this one out on
your own. As we've just discussed, failure is a pretty good teacher
and success can often be a lousy one, but as you said, you and your

team are now on the clock, with a hard and fast deadline quickly approaching."

"I don't see how my response is anything but honest. It's not that I'm downplaying our lack of results. I'm simply disagreeing with all the blame being put on my shoulders and with the decision to give us only two weeks to figure it all out," Joey replied.

"That's exactly the problem. You don't agree that the failures of your team fall squarely on *you*."

"Well, why don't you break out another one of your coins then? I'm more than willing to learn where I am falling short here!" Joey declared with a hint of irritation.

"I appreciate your humility and willingness to learn and grow. That's a commendable quality in all great leaders. But you know the rules. Only one trip a day. Besides, I'm pretty sure you wouldn't be a fan of where we would be heading," Marcus said, as he pulled out a coin and quickly flashed it Joey's way.

Joey only caught a momentary glance, but his immediate dissatisfaction was evident by his facial expression.

The coin bore the logo of the Florida Gators, one of his beloved Georgia Bulldogs' biggest rivals on the gridiron each year.

Joey's growing frustration with his lack of understanding of where he was wrong was interrupted by just how right Marcus was.

"First you make me go to Clemson. Now you're trying to take me to the Swamp," the young leader remarked, a reference to the Gators football stadium. "Looks like I dodged a bullet with your rules!"

Getting a second glance at the coin, Joey could see another unfamiliar word was inscribed underneath his rival's logo.

Ιδιοκτησία.

"I probably should have asked this before now, but what do each of these words mean?" Joey inquired.

"The Greek inscription is a reference to the historical foundations of our organization. Each word teaches a specific lesson and serves as a focal point for the journeys we take, guiding our path as leaders while never letting us forget the legacy of where we originate and the importance of upholding the **LDL** standards every day. This one stands for *ownership*, the ever-important leadership quality that is directly connected to our attitude toward failure and our ability to ultimately emulate the type of leaders we are focused on developing.

"Without ownership, you can never fully appreciate what it really means to lead, and you can never grasp the depth of responsibility that comes with the exhausting, yet wonderful burden of leadership."

"Well, no better way to burden me than having to hear about the Gators," Joey said, laughing out loud.

"Well, just bear with me on this one. This trip is about a Florida loss, so you will at least have that going for you!"

"Now that I can get on board with!"

"I know you are a college football fan, so I don't want to insult your intelligence. Do you remember The Promise?"

"You mean the speech Tim Tebow gave that was eventually put on a plaque outside the stadium?" Joey asked.

"Exactly! See, I knew you would understand the reference.

"Why don't we watch it and see what it can teach us?" Marcus said as he pulled a phone out of his pocket.

"Looks like you have the ancient **LDL** iPhone relic too," Joey declared.

"Yes, of course. After all, we are still trying to make 'tools for the mind that advance humankind.' Our tool just happens to be better leaders," Marcus said with a laugh.[1]

Joey looked perplexed.

"It's a throwback to their...ah, never mind. Let's just get back

---

1. Lund, Emily. "What Small Business Owners Can Learn from Apple's Current and Former Mission Statements." *Business Mag.* 27 Jul 2017. *https://businessingmag.com/5252/strategy/learn-from-apples-mission-statement/*. Accessed 18 May 2018.

to The Promise that would go down in Gator lore," the old man said with a look that indicated just how ancient he actually felt as the reference fell flat.

A tearful Tim Tebow, the junior quarterback for the Gators who had already been a part of one National Championship and had become the first sophomore to win the Heisman Trophy the year before, stepped to the microphone to discuss the loss his team had just suffered.

"To the fans and everybody in Gator Nation, I'm sorry. I'm extremely sorry. We were hoping for an undefeated season. That was my goal, something Florida has never done here. I promise you one thing: a lot of good will come out of this. You will never see any player in the entire country play as hard as I will play the rest of the season. You will never see someone push the rest of the team as hard as I will push everybody the rest of the season. You will never see a team play harder than we will the rest of the season. God Bless."[2]

"Reminds me of our trip to Gettysburg," Joey remarked.

"Although quite a different setting," Marcus replied.

"I just meant that he didn't need much time to clarify his thoughts. Short, sweet, and to the point, just like Lincoln's address."

"How much do you remember about this game?" Marcus asked.

"I don't remember much—mostly just how dominant the Gators team was that season and how much of an upset it was to lose to an unranked Ole Miss squad."

"Yes, this was a team that wanted to do something that had never been done at Florida before. They knew they were capable of a National Championship, but they thought they had the makings of a team that could run the table and go undefeated in the

2. NBC Sports. "Tebow 'Promise' Speech Now Memorialized." NBC Sports. 18 Mar 2009. *https://collegefootballtalk.nbcsports.com/2009/03/18/tebow-promise-speech-now-memorialized/*. Accessed 18 May 2018.

process. They had blown out their opponents to this point, and after this 31-30 loss, they would defeat the remainder of their foes by an average of thirty-five points, using Tebow's words as motivation to achieve their goal of a National Championship, even if it wasn't an undefeated one.

"What did you notice about what he said?"

"Well, first he was apologetic. He was clearly emotional about the loss. He spoke about the good that would come out of the defeat. And he seemed to feel he was the only one responsible for the loss, promising that no one would work harder than him, and in turn, his team, the rest of the season," Joey answered.

"But what about his mention of kicker Jonathan Phillips having an extra point blocked? That one point would have meant the game was tied. And what about his remarks about Major Wright getting beat deep for an eighty-six-yard touchdown? The fumble by Percy Harvin? His offensive line's collapse on that final play?"[3]

"OK, I see what you are doing here," Joey quipped.

"Tebow believed that his lack of leadership in that game was the reason they lost. He said that the team took its 'foot off the gas,' and it was up to him, one of the leaders on that team, to make sure they played each and every day up to their standard.[4] You see, this speech would become immortalized for the Gators, placed on a plaque before the next season as you mentioned, and it continues to serve as a symbol for each and every player that has worn the uniform since then.[5] But it's about more than just emotions and words. It's not just a guarantee that came to fruition with a National Championship. This is about what it means to be

3. Associated Press. "Tebow, teammates reflect on 2008 loss to Ole Miss, Promise." *USA Today.* 2 Oct 2015. *https://www.usatoday.com/story/sports/ncaaf/2015/10/02/tebow-teammates-reflect-on-2008-loss-to-ole-miss-promise/73192500/.* Accessed 18 May 2018.
4. Thompson, Edgar. "Tim Tebow's Promise speech inspires current Gators as Ole Miss returns to Swamp." *Orlando Sentinel.* 29 Sep 2015. *http://www.orlandosentinel.com/sports/nfl/os-tim-tebow-gators-promise-0930-20150929-story.html.* Accessed 18 May 2018.
5. Ibid.

a leader who is focused on the team. This is about what it means to be a leader who takes full ownership of everything he is responsible for.

"Selfish leaders will take any opportunity to deflect blame, to ensure that their reputation remains intact and everyone knows exactly where the other team members fell short, and this is directly connected to how they view failure.

"If you are afraid of failure because it's going to make you look bad or perhaps force you to sacrifice what you have worked so hard to gain, then you will never embrace the necessity of taking responsibility for everything and everyone under your leadership.

"Ownership is the natural outcome of a life spent committing to and cultivating the proper attitude toward failure. When you view failure as the partner to success, as a catalyst for future growth that can be turned into an ability to bring everyone up to their potential each and every day, then you are willing to take all the blame and get none of the credit, and you become a leader worth following.

"Tebow didn't blame the coaches for their play calling or anyone else for not doing their part. He realized that as their leader, like it or not, any failure they had collectively was his responsibility individually, and he showed that day what owning a worthy cause is all about.

"But this wasn't just about one day. He has made it evident consistently throughout his life that he has a proper understanding of failure. This is the same guy who made an attempt at a professional baseball career after his football career ended, even though he hadn't played the sport in any capacity since high school. Everyone told him it was a one in a million shot, that he had no chance at making it to the big leagues. A fear of failure would have told him not to even begin the journey. But he is a man deeply rooted in purpose, and from that purpose came a dream. He had a vision of how he could realize that dream, he believed in himself, and he was committed to the process of seeing it through. He continues to lead a life with a proper understanding of the connection between failure and success, and the result of that is a level of ownership most leaders never realize.

"I remember back in my Navy days we had a pilot in our Squadron who had nearly collided with a ship on a routine mission. Afterward he called a meeting with all the other pilots in the command to explain his failure and take ownership for what was nearly a disaster under his watch.

"He hoped that it would serve as a wake-up call for everyone else not to take their own "feet off the gas", to not become complacent with the standards that were required to accomplish the mission day in and day out. He wasn't concerned about his own failure or how it would be perceived; he just wanted to help everyone else get better.

"As he was sharing his story, one of the other pilots interrupted him to ask why he was sharing this with us. Before he could respond, the inquiring mind told all of us that he never shared his mistakes with anyone. He said he kept them all to himself because he didn't want anything to impact his reputation in the Squadron and his chance at future promotion or assignments. He wanted to appear perfect, incapable of making a mistake, but all he really did was show the rest of us that all he cared about was himself and that at the end of the day, we couldn't trust him to actually lead us anywhere."

"It's not that I'm trying to hide my failures," Joey said, interrupting Marcus. "I'm not afraid to admit when I am wrong; I just don't see how this is all my fault."

"*You* are the leader," Marcus said. "Everything that happens on your team is your responsibility. It may not always seem fair, but that's what it means to lead. The moment you start deflecting blame back toward Bill or the board or anyone else is the moment you begin to lose the influence you have worked so hard to gain."

"Man, I tell you what, I'm learning more and more every day just how tough this whole leadership thing really is," Joey commented with a sigh.

"You better believe it! Leadership is exhausting!" Marcus declared enthusiastically.

"Mediocre leaders, leaders who don't focus on purpose or vision or standards or belief or commitment or discipline or embrace failure, they have it easy. It doesn't require anything of you to just sit back and take all the praise and deflect all the criticism. But great leaders believe that in the end, it's not about *you*.

"In the end, it's about the mission, it's about the worthy cause and those you are leading, and when you understand that, it causes you to choose to accept responsibility for everything that happens on your watch as a leader. You can't help but take ownership when your own status is no longer a factor, when you are focused on bringing everyone else up to their highest potential. Great leaders understand the daily process needed for them to continuously achieve a life of excellence and help others to do the same. They know what's required, and they know that even after all the effort, all the struggle, and all the pain, in the end, they are going to give away all the credit and shoulder all the blame."

"That's just crazy sounding!" Joey exclaimed.

"Well, here's the craziest part. Great leaders wouldn't want it any other way! They embrace it! When you actually learn to establish a mindset of being others-focused, you want nothing more than to see those around you succeed, and that's the beauty of the burden of leadership. In the end, it's not really a burden at all."

"OK, so even if I agree that all our failures are my responsibility, what's so wrong with disagreeing with the board's decision for the team? I can't second-guess the decisions of those above me?" Joey asked.

"Of course you can, and you should. Any leader worth following would encourage you to do so. When ego is no longer a factor, then the leader-follower relationship can thrive. You should feel empowered to speak up and offer different solutions and a better way forward. But that's a conversation between you and the board, between you and your leaders. Once the decision has been made, even if it's not the outcome you hoped for or perhaps the way you would have moved forward, you need to own that decision just as you own your responsibilities as a leader.

"Gripes go up the chain, not down. Your team gripes to you, you take your complaints to your boss, and so on and so forth. The moment you refuse to take ownership of their decision, the moment you start questioning and complaining what you are being asked to do openly in front of your team is the moment they begin to lose confidence in your ability to actually lead them. They'll start to see you as nothing more than a puppet, passing off your leadership role in the decision-making process. When this happens, the validity of your choices come under scrutiny as your followers wonder if you are even capable of making decisions on your own and leading them in the first place."

"So I'm supposed to just be OK with every decision made above me? It seems disingenuous to pretend that I'm happy with what's been decided here," Joey said.

"Now, don't misunderstand. This isn't about blindly accepting orders or decisions. It isn't about having to agree with every choice made on high. It's about how you properly communicate your concerns as a follower and how you present them to your team as their leader.

"If you have established the proper leader-follower relationship with those in charge of you, then you should feel empowered to bring up issues or propose different ways of accomplishing your mission. How you choose to handle this in your role as a follower sets the tone for how your own team will do this with you as their leader. You must set the standard with your team for how to follow just as you show them what it means to lead. This is the golden rule of leadership, after all.

"You lead how you want to be led, and you follow how you want to be followed!

"We are not always going to have the luxury of following great leaders. I know you feel that at this very moment. But at the end of the day, as *your* team's leader, you have a responsibility to set the standards that you know will lead to building your vision for the future to the proper code even if those above you aren't doing the same for you. If all your team sees is you passing the blame for every decision back to those above you, not only will they question your ability to make decisions and actually lead them, but you will be showing them that as your followers, there is no standard of individual ownership required for them either.

"It's hard to be a leader developing other leaders if you can't be a follower developing other followers!

"Own your failures. Own the board's decision as if it was yours. Present a united front. Set the example for them as both leader and follower. Embrace the two weeks you have to solve this problem as two weeks to continue calling everyone up to the life of excellence you know they are capable of living.

"Believe! Be committed! Be disciplined in your pursuit!

"Make this failure the partner to your ultimate success!

"OWN THE WORTHY CAUSE AND LEAD YOUR TEAM, JOEY!"

"OK, OK, I think I'm ready," the young leader said, interrupting the old man's passionate speech. "I need to get down to the twenty-third floor before word spreads of what is going on."

Marcus gave the young leader a hug, nodding at him in silence as he sent him on his way.

When Joey stepped off the elevator two floors below, the team was hard at work, the motivation carrying over from last week as if nothing had changed.

He had beat the news downstairs.

Joey called everyone together and shared with them the revelation that even though they had failed up to this point to find a solution, even though things had not gone according to plan, they still had two weeks to figure this whole thing out.

That opportunity, Joey said, would provide them with everything they needed to continue to get better, to realize their purpose, and see the dream achieved through the collective vision born in them over the last two months.

This was the push to the finish line, and they were going to run their race to get the prize, to do the right things in the right way at the right time for the right reasons.

He expected grumbling, another "I told you so" from Sam, or perhaps the obvious anxiety he himself was feeling at just how tall this task appeared to be, but he got none of that.

He had given the team no reason to question where this decision came from, and he had sowed no seeds of discontent. He took ownership of where they were and spoke with confidence and belief about where they were headed...and it worked.

Two months of building to this point had the team unfazed by what would have been devastating news just a few weeks earlier.

They took it all in stride as if this was nothing more than an opportunity to prove everyone else wrong, to fully exercise the standards Joey had been preaching, and to practice the disciplined pursuit of excellence they had been hearing so much about.

Joey breathed a sigh of relief. This had become a sort of virtuous circle, the team now reinforcing in Joey the belief he had been trying so hard to instill in them.

He sent them back to work, taking in their growth and willingness to put the needs of the team ahead of themselves as they returned to their desks and got right back to the collaborative task at hand.

"Leadership is exhausting, I'll give Marcus that. But moments like these, well, they make it all worth it!"

CHAPTER 9

Ελαστικότη
RESILIENCE

*"For though the righteous fall seven times, they rise
again, but the wicked stumble when calamity strikes."*

—PROVERBS 24:16

T HE NEXT TWO days were the most productive in weeks for
Joey and his team. Everyone appeared to be on board with
where they were heading and what they were trying to accomplish, and to top it all off, they were beginning to have some
breakthroughs.

There was nothing definitive yet that Joey could take back
to the boardroom, but Cathy shared some innovative ideas she
thought might satisfy the production floor, manufacturing, and
the accounting office.

It was by no means a perfect solution. A firm decision would
still have to be made that quality came above all else, even the
almighty dollar, but given the time constraints and pressure they
were under, it was something Joey and the team could run with.

For the first time since being assigned to lead his "dynamic
dozen," Joey felt a sense of confidence in his abilities to guide and
direct the team toward a vision that would accomplish the dreams
inspired by the company's purpose.

It was almost as if the brutal Monday morning meeting was
simply a lost nightmare, a memory tucked away for future refer-

ence but no longer weighing the young leader down with the burden of responsibility that paralyzed him in its aftermath. Instead, his ability to take ownership of the situation had galvanized his group.

It was astonishing to him how taking full responsibility counterintuitively removed the constraints that seemed to trap him.

As the team furiously moved forward with their plan, Ron and Sam pulled Joey aside and asked if they could take him out to lunch. Joey hesitated for a moment since the team had a ton of work to accomplish, but he also knew that even as they were pressed against an impossible deadline, it was his job to continue building intentional, authentic relationships.

And that's what he genuinely wanted to do. He was no longer trying to get to know them because he felt he had to in order to lead them. He was becoming deeply passionate about the opportunity he had as their leader to call them a place he knew they were capable of going. So he jumped at the chance to spend time with them while eating a hot meal.

As any good Georgians would do, they decided to head to Chick-fil-A, the Atlanta-based exemplar of southern hospitality and service that is unmatched in the quick-service sector. Conveniently, the closest server of chicken coated and fried in peanut oil was only a half a block away from the office.

As the three men made their way down the street, Joey began to think more about the southern staple. Here was a company founded and guided by an unwavering purpose.

As they entered the restaurant, that purpose was on display for everyone to see: "to glorify God by being a faithful steward of all that is entrusted to us and to have a positive influence on all that come into contact with Chick-fil-A".[1]

Clearly, Chick-fil-A has purpose-inspired dreams connected by a vision built on standards of quality and service. They seek

---

1. "Who We Are." *Chick-Fil-A*, www.chick-fil-a.com/About/Who-We-Are.

operational excellence and consistently crave-able food while taking customer service to the next level by constantly striving to go the "second mile" with their guests.

And to top it all off, they are closed on Sundays, refusing to sacrifice their beliefs and values for the sake of making a profit.

It isn't like they are hurting for money either, Joey thought, chuckling to himself. He knew that Chick-fil-A had the highest per store sales average of any restaurant in the country. They were open nearly 20 percent less a week and brought in more than double the revenue per store than their next closest competitor.[2] *That's truly a remarkable accomplishment, and one centered on a foundation of living out what is most important to you*, he thought.

Joey decided this would be another guiding light for him as he sought to change his thinking about what it really means to lead. It was a weird feeling for him, too—drawing inspiration from others in a way that was completely foreign to him just a few weeks ago. He wasn't sure if this was all a part of Marcus' master plan, but he couldn't argue with the results.

He was becoming more observant of the lessons the old man had instilled in him, seeing positive examples emerge all around him as he tried to implement these same traits in his own life and with his own team.

His thoughts were interrupted by a team member bringing their food to the table. As was the customary encounter at Chick-fil-A, smiles were present, eye contact was made, and a hearty "my pleasure" was given at the end.

Joey attempted to continue discussing the plan they had decided to move forward with while consuming his waffle fries, but Ron and Sam seemed suddenly distant. The young leader could sense that something was off.

"You guys alright? I know the food is good and all, but I really

---

2. McCreary, Matthew. "Chick-Fil-A Makes More Per Restaurant Than McDonald's, Starbucks and Subway Combined ... and It's Closed on Sundays." *Entrepreneur*, 30 Mar. 2019, www.entrepreneur.com/article/320615.

want to hear what you two think of our plan. It's not perfect, I know, but we will ensure as many people remain on the production floor as possible and work to cross-train others to operate the new machinery. And we should get our production levels back to being stable without having to fully shut down the manufacturing process in order to upgrade.

"Now, I know that's still a big ask for you, but we have to meet the standard of quality we promise our customers. You saw the pilots that are in need of proper functioning equipment first-hand. We can't let those brave young men and women down—we just can't!"

"Joey, Joey," Sam broke in, cutting him off mid-sentence. "Let me stop you right there. We...we have something to tell you," he continued, stammering to get the words out and refusing to look Joey in the eye. Instead, he looked over at Ron, who gave him a reassuring nod.

"Joey, we have to quit the team effective immediately. We want to be reassigned back to our regular jobs and get back to our normal work."

Joey was shaken to his core.

"What do you mean you have to quit the team?" he exclaimed. "That's not your call to make!"

"Actually, it's kind of already been made," Ron said, joining the conversation. "You see, Bill pretty much told us we didn't have a choice. We both explained to him that even though you were approaching things quite differently than we were accustomed to, there was a chance we would solve this thing once and for all, but he wasn't buying it. He told us you were a lame-duck leader and there was no way you were going to survive after the next two weeks. He said that if we wanted to keep our jobs, it was in our best interest to make our way out of the corporate headquarters and back to the manufacturing floor."

"We wanted to be upfront with you about this because of the way you have treated us the past several months," Sam said. "You have been like a breath of fresh air! I really mean that. You know how unsure I was in the beginning, but please don't think this is because of something you did. You have really made us question the way we have always done things, and to be honest, we both buy into what you have been preaching. But regardless of how this turns out, Bill is our boss. We both have families to think of, and we can't afford to put that at risk right now. We just felt that, after everything you have done to help us the last two months, we owed you the truth, not some second-hand rumor passed around the office by everyone else."

Joey was in complete shock. He sank down in his booth and pushed his tray away from him.

"Guys, I'm not asking you to pick sides between me and Bill. We are all supposed to be on the same team here. I'm just asking you to believe in my vision enough to commit to this team for twelve more days. Just twelve more days! You can't leave us hanging in the home stretch."

"There are still representatives from the production floor," Ron reminded him.

"Yeah, you still have Liz and Steve," Sam added.

"We really are sorry, and I promise you, we hope you and the team prove everyone wrong," Ron said, as the two men stood up and walked toward the door. "No one is cheering harder for you than we are."

Joey put his head in his hands and closed his eyes.

"After all we've been through the last two months and all I've poured into their lives, they are just going to quit on me?" he said softly.

"Can I refresh your beverage?" he heard someone ask.

"Marcus? You work at Chick-fil-A?"

"I wouldn't say I work for them," the old man responded. "I just enjoy serving others, and it looks like you could use a little more sweet tea."

Joey nodded in agreement, allowing his mentor to refill his cup, and then proceeded to break the news about what had just transpired.

"We were finally making progress and now this?" the young leader said in summary.

"Sounds like you really made a difference in their lives in a short time!"

"That's what you're taking away from what just happened? It's been one thing after another and Bill completely has it out for me, but hey, at least they like me?"

"I'm sorry. I don't mean to be rude. I just really thought my breakthrough was coming."

Marcus stopped the young man dead in his tracks. "We've been over this. It isn't about you. None of this is about you. Sometimes, it's about planting seeds you will never see. You made a difference in the lives of those two men in the short time you got to spend with them. If you're worried about how this affects you or what you stand to gain or lose, you're missing the whole point."

"I really didn't mean to make this about me. But it's hard to separate their decision from a failure on my part to get them to fully commit. And to be honest, it's tough to keep going, to walk back into the office with a smile on my face after another round in the ring when I've been bloodied and bruised as their leader."

While Joey was talking, Marcus had turned to the table next to him and was offering mints to the guests. He turned back toward the young leader and reached in his pocket once again.

"No thank you!" Joey said, motioning the old man's offer away with his hand.

Instead of a piece of candy, however, Marcus pulled out a coin and set it on the table.

"You sure?"

Joey instantaneously felt a sense of relief, that somehow Marcus was going to steer him in the right direction again, coupled with an overwhelming concern that at the end of the day, none of this was going to matter for him and his team.

"This one is tough to experience," Marcus declared, leaving the decision to commence the journey up to the young man.

Joey sat there for a moment, staring at the coin facing up at him, uncertain whether he was prepared for what was on the other side. The shining reflection was glittering on the table, daring him to take the next step in his leadership journey.

He looked at the coin, a picture of a compass adorning its front, with the word Ελαστικότη etched below.

He reached for the coin, but Marcus scooped it up before he had a chance. "Best let me take the lead on this one. I just wanted to make sure you were willing."

With that, the old man threw the coin up into the air, the two of them emerging from the blinding light into the fading sunset barely shining through the trees of their new surroundings on the wet ground below.

Ahead of them, Joey could make out the shadow of a man lying on the jungle floor, motionless and unconscious, his slow and steady breathing the only sign that he was alive.

Without hesitating or looking for affirmation from his mentor, the young leader crawled over to the unconscious individual and assessed the situation around him.

As he got closer to the man, it became evident that he was badly injured. His clothing gave away his profession.

A tattered flight suit, worn and ripped apart meant he was an aviator of some kind who had survived a crash and landed in this dense grouping of trees.

His hand appeared broken in several places, his fingers tied back in a crumpled mess, held together by some strands of his shredded flight suit. His leg was broken as well—not merely displaced but the bone completely snapped off. A makeshift tourniquet had been applied to keep it as straight as possible.

Joey felt nauseous at the sight of the injuries. As he continued to take note of the helpless condition of the man on the ground in front of him, the sounds of the jungle dissipated as an aircraft flew overhead.

He could hear voices near them, and suddenly the badly wounded man sat up and reached for his radio as the aircraft overhead searched for his position.

"AWOL 1 Bravo," the young pilot said calmly. "I'm hurt bad. Compound fracture. My head's hurt too. I've been in and out of consciousness for the last day."

"Who is the greatest football team in the world?" was the response on the radio.

"The Green Bay Packers," said the pilot.[3]

Joey looked at Marcus, a bit puzzled at the question. This didn't seem like the time for NFL rivalry talk.

"They're just confirming his identity. Standard practice," the old man explained.

The pilot pulled a syringe from his pocket and injected himself, attempting to subdue some of the pain he felt.

The sun continued to set; it was nearly gone from the horizon when the radio chatter started once again.

"Drop the penetrator," came a voice on the radio.

"Negative!" replied the young pilot. "The enemy is surrounding us. Drop it where you are, and I'll crawl to you."

Joey was perplexed. Instead of allowing the rescuers to come to him, the pilot who could barely move was going to crawl to them just to ensure their safety?

As the young pilot gave all he had to crawl across the jungle floor, enemy fire erupted through the trees. He inched closer until

---

3. Stockdale, James B. *Thoughts of a Philosophical Fighter Pilot*: 431 (Hoover Institution Press Publication). Hoover Institution Press. Kindle Edition.

he was almost there, mere feet from rescue with the sounds of gunfire echoing louder all around them.

Joey knew nothing could hurt him, but it was still a terrifying experience. He wanted to scream for the young man, to cheer him on to victory as he gave every last measure of effort he had and was rescued. But just as he was about to make it, the chopper above pulled away; the enemy fire evidently too great for them to wait around any longer.

Joey shouted in disbelief. "Why wouldn't the pilot let them come to him?"

As the pilot continued to crawl across the tree roots back out of sight of the enemy, he began to wonder why Marcus had wanted him to see this attempted rescue. Was it so he would realize that what he was going through really wasn't that bad?

He turned toward Marcus, attempting to grab the coin and head back to Atlanta.

"This isn't the end of the journey," declared the old man. "This is only the beginning."

Marcus tossed the coin in the air, and they emerged once again on the jungle floor in the dead of night. As Joey scanned his surroundings, he noticed the young pilot again. His beard and hair were now noticeably longer. His body was much more emaciated and weak, but his countenance appeared untouched by his situation.

Joey wasn't sure how many days had passed, but the young pilot continued to trudge along, ignoring his thirst and hunger, willing himself further down the path toward what he hoped was an eventual escape.

While he continued inching along and evading the enemy, Joey looked to Marcus to fill in the gaps of what he was witnessing.

"This is Captain Lance P. Sijan," explained the old man. "A Midwestern boy and a football player at the Air Force Academy, chosen by his fellow cadets as the toughest in his graduating class.[4] He was shot down over Laos in November 1967. You saw his decision to wave off a rescue so that others would not be put in harm's way.[5] What you haven't seen is that over the last forty-five days, Lance P. Sijan has experienced more failure, more disappointment, and more obstacles than any man could ever hope to overcome."

"Forty-five days?" Joey said in disbelief, not sure he had heard Marcus correctly.

"Yes. For forty-five days, he has overcome a dismembered hand and leg and a terrible head injury. He has overcome hunger and thirst with the will to continue overtaking his need for nutrients. He has overcome the bouts of unconsciousness and the inability to maintain a rational state of being. He has overcome falling into an abandoned French latrine and being stuck there for days, unconscious and unable to escape. And do you know what his attitude was toward the sinkhole where he found himself?"

"I can't even begin to imagine where my mind would go in that situation," Joey responded.

"He was grateful!

"He was grateful, because once he climbed out, he discovered that the North Vietnamese had been searching that area for days and more than likely would have found him. Falling in a pit of broken sewer pipes was a blessing to Captain Sijan.[6] He then crawled on his belly for weeks on end, sometimes inching himself forward a mere 100 yards a day.

"He was in an impossible situation, but still, he was moving forward, having evaded capture for a month and a half in the worst conditions imaginable. He found water, leeches, bugs, and berries. He became keenly aware that he was only going to be able to think clearly for an hour or two a day and needed to maximize his rational state of being.[7] Along the way, he lost his gun, strobe

---

4. Ibid, Location 3201.
5. Ibid, Location 3210.
6. Ibid, Location 3295.
7. Ibid, Location 3295.

light, and radio. The loss of those three objects would have broken a lesser man, but not Captain Sijan. No, he still had his compass, and he was still headed east towards escape!"[8]

Joey thought back to the inscription of the compass on the coin as he looked down at a weary Captain Sijan, beaten down but not dejected, aware of the severity of his situation but refusing to give up on himself or his fellow airmen.

"And here he is, barely able to move, on Christmas Eve 1967," Marcus continued. "Tomorrow morning, on Christmas Day, he will pass out on the Ho Chi Minh trail, forty-six days since he ejected from his aircraft, and he will be captured by the North Vietnamese.[9] It had taken him forty-six days to travel a total of three miles.

"He will somehow manage to find it within himself to overcome a guard and escape once again, before being recaptured nearly a day later. He will be tortured for nine days, a shell of the man he once was on the outside, but with an unbreakable will on the inside. He won't give up anything to his captors. He will remain within the Code of Conduct, divulging only his name, rank, and serial number until the very end.

"Incredibly, he will never complain to his fellow prisoners about his predicament. He will continue to talk positively about the future, aware of just how dire his circumstances are yet full of the faith that he will make it through. He will remain loyal to his country, loyal to its cause, and loyal to his fellow service members until his last breath.

"On January 22, 1968, Captain Lance P. Sijan will pass away, and for his willingness to go above and beyond the call of duty, to do more than could ever be expected of an individual in his circumstances, he will be posthumously awarded the Congres-

---

8. "Unbroken Will: The Captain Lance P. Sijan Story." *DVIDS*, www.dvidshub.net/video/562381/unbroken-will-captain-lance-p-sijan-story.

9. Stockdale, James B. *Thoughts of a Philosophical Fighter Pilot*: 431 (Hoover Institution Press Publication). Hoover Institution Press. Kindle Edition.

sional Medal of Honor—the first Air Force Academy graduate to receive the award."

With that, Marcus motioned Joey to look at Captain Sijan one final time, allowing the young leader to fully embed the image of the hero in his brain before flipping the coin and returning to the Chick-fil-A booth in Atlanta.

Joey, in what had become a ritual at this point, was at a loss for words.

Marcus chimed in. "Here, have a drink, son," the old man said, encouraging the young leader to take a sip of the sweet tea he had refreshed what seemed like hours ago.

"I just don't understand how someone could keep going through an experience like that," Joey said. "I mean, to keep crawling, inch after inch, hour after hour, day after day, week after week, with broken bones, a weakened body, and no food or water. I just can't fathom it. And then, at the end of it all, to never give in, to still believe that your circumstances will get better...that takes a level of resolve unlike any I've ever seen or comprehended in my life."

"You know, it's funny," Marcus said, "James Stockdale, the senior Naval officer and one of the most prominent Prisoners of War in the famed Hoa Lo Prison in Vietnam, spoke at great lengths about that word *resolve*. After spending seven and a half years as a POW, routinely tortured, kept in isolation for years, locked in leg irons for weeks at a time, Stockdale, like Sijan, found his time as a prisoner a blessing. It tested his resolve, and what he found was that the most important value, the thing that mattered most to Stockdale—and the one he communicated down to everyone in the prison through their tap code system—was love for the 'guy next door.'[10] For Stockdale, the leader of the resistance within the Hanoi Hilton, 'resolve [was] too expensive to waste

---

10. Ibid, Location 1011.

on trivial things and too precious to throw away on anything you don't believe to your bones to be worthy of you.'[11]

"This is why it all starts for us with purpose. Spending yourself in a worthy cause, a cause you and your team are called to fulfill. A cause that is grounded in proper values and brings you and those you lead to their own *eudaimonic* flourishing. A cause that is worthy of your resolve. When that occurs, you can 'learn to use [the] fire for what it was intended, a flame that cauterizes your will to make you stronger next time.'[12]

"Captain Sijan's resolve went beyond what we could reasonably expect from an individual. It was grounded in love for his brother next door. It was rooted in a dedication to his country. It led to an unwillingness to give in to anything or break the code for which he stood for."

"How can I possibly find in myself that level of resolve and determination?" Joey asked. "You've seen it firsthand. I'm on a roller coaster of highs and lows, unable to weather the storms of leadership. My bridge is definitely not CAVU at the moment."

"You know, Vice Admiral Stockdale was a big fan of stoicism. He was a connoisseur of ancient philosophers such as Epictetus and Aristotle, and he believed 'it is not the what but the how. It is not the result, but the spirit with which you pursue your just ends that really counts.'[13]

"Aristotle believed that in order to achieve *arete*, to live a life of true excellence, we must habituate the virtues of life, that which is always good. We must first know what is virtuous, but in order to become virtuous, we must *act* on what is virtuous. He would say that 'we become builders by building, and we become harpists by playing the harp. Similarly, then, we become just by doing just actions.' Part of the way we do that is by identifying those virtues exhibited in others, and by allowing those men and women to

---

11. Ibid, Location 1079.
12. Ibid, Location 1286.
13. Ibid, Location 1518.

serve as our moral exemplars in life. That's why we're here. That's why **LDL** exists. These coins provide nothing more than the opportunity to see what a life of virtue is supposed to look like, to have a roadmap and the guideposts of the moral exemplars who came before us."

"OK, but even if that's the case, how do I take what we just witnessed and turn it into something I can habituate, something I can grow to possess as well?" Joey asked.

"I think at this moment, when you're facing another difficult test with your team, you have the chance to do just that," the old man said. "Epictetus and the Stoics believed that the invincible man is the one who cannot be dismayed by anything that happens beyond his control.[14] There are things within your power, and there are circumstances beyond your power. You control the input, and you let the output take care of itself. You control you!

"Our discussion on discipline at the golf course applies to every aspect of who you are, including your thoughts. What you think, how you think, and your ability to find the good in the bad, just like Captain Sijan and Vice Admiral Stockdale, is part of the process of creating a life of resilience.

"To the Stoic, the greatest injury that can be inflicted on a person is not the one that comes at the hands of torture. It is the injury that can only be administered by himself when he destroys the good man within him."[15]

Joey felt like he was catching on. "So, keep going back to my purpose, make sure my cause is worthy, control what I can control, become disciplined in my thoughts, and ensure that I am upholding the values that I espouse through my actions each and every day?"

Marcus beamed with pride. The lessons were tough on his young protégé, but he was learning what it meant to lead.

"Napoleon said, 'In war, the moral is to the physical as three is

---

14. Ibid, Location 4778.
15. Ibid, Location 3625.

to one.' Shortcomings and failures in plans and techniques can be overcome, but [moral failures] in a leader are catastrophic."[16]

You don't need the resiliency of Captain Sijan. But you do need to understand the importance of resolve in your life and the leader you are working desperately to become for the sake of your team. And you must start your own long journey of action, just like Lance P. Sijan did. Each day you should be crawling forward, inch by inch, a little more resolute, keeping your head down, making intentional decisions that move you toward the leader you want to become. It's not enough to merely know what is virtuous. You must *act*! Your cause is worthy, my friend. You want what is best for the company and your team.

"Now it's time to follow that up with a level of resolve, resilience, and determination that measures up to that purpose."

---

16. Ibid, Location 4129.

CHAPTER 10

σκέψη

REFLECTION

"Give me six hours to chop down a tree and I will spend the first four sharpening the axe."

—ABRAHAM LINCOLN

THE CHALLENGE HAD been issued.

Joey was thankful for Marcus' guidance and wisdom. The lesson in resiliency and resolve was one that targeted who he was deep down in his soul and made him consider all the actions it would take to become excellent in Aristotle's eyes.

Now, more than ever, the emerging young leader felt as though everything his team was enduring would push them forward to a resolution. They would control what they could control over the remaining time they had together.

The rest of the week was spent in a sort of orchestrated chaos, not unlike the time Joey had spent aboard the *Sammy B*. His remaining team members were focused on the task at hand, moving about with unregulated precision, the ideas flowing as the finish line drew closer.

Joey hadn't really stopped to consider how the team was only a few days away from wrapping up their time together. A little over a week from now, regardless of their successes and failures, they would move back to their own departments. Joey wondered what impact, if any, he would have made on them.

He felt that he had made a difference, but he also felt as though he had been so consumed with how much he had to grow personally as a leader that he had at times neglected his responsibility to grow his team.

Friday came and went, and the team left for the weekend knowing that on Monday they would compile their solution, spending the final week working like crazy to dot the i's and cross the t's in preparation for Joey's meeting with the board.

As he headed to his car to make the trek up the interstate to his apartment in Buckhead, he reflected on the entire experience. He thought back to his first encounter with Marcus, who seemed to know from the first moment they met that he had something to offer the young leader and who was always, always looking for a way to serve him.

He considered all the little breadcrumbs dropped along the way by his new mentor, and he started to understand some of the mystery surrounding the **LDL** organization.

Marcus said it's very literal: Leaders Developing Leaders. That's the goal, Joey thought. *I've been making significant strides at becoming the type of leader worth following, but I'm not sure I've done much of anything to become a leader that develops other leaders. I mean, I barely understood what was required of me as a leader until the past couple of weeks. Heck, all I've really done is continuously be reminded of just how much further I have to go as a leader myself. Still, I can't help but feeling deep down that I'll never really be fulfilled until I'm able to pass along what I've learned and help others become the best versions of themselves as well.*

Joey's phone suddenly dinged as an incoming text message appeared on his screen.

"Bingo!" was all it said.

"Oh, come on!" Joey shouted. "What, do you have some kind of tracking device on my car that listens in on my conversations with myself?"

"Hey, you told me that I needed to work on not startling you," came a reply from the backseat.

Joey looked back, nearly crossing the median and wrecking his car.

"Best to keep that windshield mentality and focus on what's in front of you," Marcus added.

"Geez! The text message was nice and all, but randomly appearing in someone's car is always going to startle someone who began their drive alone!" Joey shouted.

Marcus took out a notebook and pen from his pocket and began to jot down something.

Text message prior not enough. Need to reevaluate my assumptions on what will and what won't startle.

"What are you doing?" Joey asked.

"Oh, just taking note of your observation, making sure I give it the proper reflection this weekend."

"I'm not even going to ask at this point how you got in my car?"

"Why not? Is that something you are curious to find out?"

"Well, I mean, yeah, but given every wild and impossible moment you have been able to conjure up, I've just decided I'm either certifiably crazy or in need of a CT scan on my brain after this project is complete."

"That's quite the interesting assumption. You haven't once thought to ask about it, though?"

"Of course I have! It's just not possible, so I must be crazy, right?"

"Kind of like your situation at work?"

"Well, yeah, but ..."

"And what assumptions have you made in deciding the inevitability of your predicament with your team?"

"Well, I haven't really thought about any specific assumptions," Joey responded. "Let's go back a minute because I can tell you are about to share something with me, but first why were you making a note about my reaction to you showing up here unannounced?"

"It's pretty simple, really. I spend time each day thinking about thinking!"

"Thinking about thinking? Is that some kind of **LDL** slogan or something?"

"No, that's straight from Marcus. I take time each day to think about how I think."

"It's the story of my life lately it seems, but I'm confused here," Joey retorted. "I barely have time each day to think about all the things I have to get done. I couldn't possibly find time to think about how I think."

"And what were you just doing before I interrupted you?" Marcus replied. "You were reflecting on your experiences, realizing the importance of being a leader who pours himself into the lives of others and develops other leaders. Are you telling me you can't find time to think on the ride home from work?"

"I mean, I usually just like to listen to music and relax from the tough days at the office," Joey answered.

"So, you have time. You just don't understand its importance? Well, don't just take my word for it. How about we see how one of the world's most successful businessmen thinks?" Marcus said as he opened his briefcase and pulled out another coin.

Since he was driving, Joey couldn't look back and see what was engraved on this one. Instead, he put on his turn signal so he could pull off the highway and stop the car.

Marcus simply said, "No need," as he gave the coin a toss and Joey joined his mentor in the back seat of someone else's automobile.

For once, the old man did not give Joey a chance to gather his surroundings before explaining where they had journeyed and why they were there.

"We are riding to work with Mr. Warren Buffett today."

"THE Warren Buffett?" Joey exclaimed. "The Oracle of Omaha? The greatest investor of our time?"

"One and the same!" Marcus responded.

"Oh man, this is going to be good!" Joey declared as Mr. Buffett pulled up to a McDonald's and ordered breakfast.

As Warren Buffett drove around to the drive-thru window, exact change in hand, Joey found it odd that one of the richest men in the world would drive himself to work and stop at a McDonald's along the way.

"Couldn't he just have someone chauffeur him around and pick up his fast-food orders for him?" he asked Marcus.

"Routine is important to Mr. Buffett. I'm sure as a former athlete, you understand the need for routine."

"Yes, absolutely! I did the same warm-up routine for years before every game."

"Well, it's the same here. Not that we should become stuck in our ways, but no matter how big or small, the process for achieving and sustaining success remains constant."

They pulled into the parking lot of Berkshire Hathaway and followed the billionaire businessman up to his office.

The Omaha legend did not sit down at his computer and begin cranking out emails. In fact, Joey didn't see a computer on his desk at all. He didn't pick up the phone or start looking at his calendar to see what was on tap for the day.

Instead, he sat down, ate his Sausage, Egg, and Cheese McGriddle, and began reading the paper.[1] He moved from one paper to the next, for what seemed like hours on end.

After that, he moved onto financial reports, combing through every single detail of the company he was researching, never so much as breaking eye contact with the page, let alone being distracted by anything else going on in the world.

It was clear to Joey that he was laser-focused, but there wasn't much here to see. There was nothing glamorous or flashy about his "process."

---

1. "Documentaries Catalog." *HBO*, www.hbo.com/documentaries/catalog.becoming-warren-buffett.

"So, that's it? We came here to watch him eat McDonald's and read the paper?" he asked Marcus.

"Pretty much," the old man replied. "You see, Mr. Buffett has explained that the single greatest factor in his success is focus. When he met Bill Gates for the first time, they sat down and each wrote down the word that was most important to them, and they wrote down the exact same word: focus.[2] Mr. Buffett estimates that he has spent 80 percent of his career simply reading and thinking.[3]

"He believes that critical thinking—taking the time to really think about and consider every option, alternative, assumption, bias, implication, and consequence—is critical to his success. He literally spends the majority of his day thinking about thinking, ensuring that he has the proper information to make the informed decisions he needs to make as the chairman of the fourth-largest company in the country. His entire calendar is built around the idea of intentional thinking!"[4]

"Wow! I never really considered the importance of setting aside time to yourself to simply think as an option," Joey observed. "In our fast-paced world, it seems like if you take a second away from focusing on the work at hand, someone else is coming along that will overtake you."

"Taking time to think allows you to make the best decisions possible," Marcus replied. "You've been running around as the leader of your team like a chicken with your head cut off the last couple of months. What if you simply took the time to challenge some of your assumptions, to make sure you had the information necessary to make the most informed decision possible?

"Here's the thing. It's not just that Mr. Buffett is passively reading or thinking. He's literally scheduling the time to be deliberate

2. Ibid.
3. Empact. "Why Successful People Spend 10 Hours a Week Just Thinking." *Inc.com*, Inc., 7 Apr. 2016, www.inc.com/empact/why-successful-people-spend-10-hours-a-week-just-thinking.html.
4. Ibid.

in analyzing the information he is consuming, to make sure he can form his own insights from what he is evaluating."[5]

"That's just not something you see often in today's corporate world," Joey exclaimed.

"No, it isn't. But reflection and critical thinking are crucial to your ability to find sustained success, to ensure you are living up to your own version of *arete*. I'm not talking only about finding success in business, either. I'm talking about analyzing down to the smallest detail who you are becoming as a leader and the things you are pursuing."

"Wait, so now it's not just about making smart business choices? I also have to spend time thinking about thinking with regards to my leadership too?"

"Without a doubt!" Marcus said emphatically.

Joey looked at Mr. Buffett again, still entranced with the financial reports he was thumbing through. "He seems to know more about most companies than those companies know about themselves," he commented.

"He has a habit, a consistency of action, that he developed as a young man that has carried him to the pinnacle of business and investing," Marcus responded. "He takes the long view. He approaches his investing like Ted Williams approached hitting, looking at thousands of companies and waiting patiently for one in his sweet spot that he could hit out of the park."[6]

"So how do I implement this in my life, in my role as a leader?" Joey interrupted.

"First, you have to decide that this is important to you! You have to become a believer in the power of reflection and critical thinking and make up your mind that you are going to spend time each day evaluating who you are becoming and the decisions you

---

5. Hill, Denise. "Why Critical Thinking Is Crucial to Your Success and How to Improve It." *Lifehack*, Lifehack, 24 Apr. 2017, www.lifehack.org/572725/why-critical-thinking-essential-your-success-and-how-you-can-improve.

6. "Documentaries Catalog." *HBO*, www.hbo.com/documentaries/catalog.becoming-warren-buffett.

are making as a leader. If it's important to you, you will take the time to habituate it through daily action. After all, as Mr. Buffett often says, 'the chains of habit are too light to be felt until they are too heavy to be broken.'[7] Who you are becoming is directly dependent on your willingness to spend time thinking about the way you think."

"Okay, so let's say I decide that I need to reevaluate the way I think. How do I put that into action? And how do I learn to do this in a way I can then pass on to the leaders I'm developing?"

"I love that your focus has become centered around bettering yourself so you can, in turn, bring out the best in others," Marcus said with a smile. "Critical thinking, just like your resolve, just like all the other habits you are creating, is a process, not an outcome. There's no end result. It is a process of refining how you think, of identifying and challenging your assumptions, of imagining and exploring alternatives. The better you become at the process, the better you become at thinking, the better you become as a leader.

"You need to always be bringing it back to your purpose, focusing your attention on attacking the most pertinent questions at hand. You have to gather as much information as you have the time to gather. This can only be done if you are asking the right questions and ensuring you have the right information. You need to check your inferences and assumptions. You must clarify the concepts you are using to evaluate the information you've obtained. You need to understand the point of view you are using to address your thinking. We all come at questions from different angles, but understanding your point of view and considering other points of view, especially when coupled with a willingness to check your assumptions, leads to a clearer picture of the way forward. Finally, you need to think through as many implications as possible before arriving at a conclusion."[8]

---

7. Ibid.
8. Elder, Linda, and Richard Paul. *The Thinker's Guide to Analytic Thinking*. The Foundation for Critical Thinking, 2012.

"Okay, let's go back for a second," Joey said. "How do I make sure I'm gaining the right information?"

"I would challenge you to make sure you have the proper level of clarity and accuracy in your data. Don't just assume the information you are getting is clear and accurate. Make sure the information is precise and relevant to the decision you are trying to make. Make sure you have the appropriate depth and breadth as well. It's not just about taking in tons of information. It's about taking in the *right* information.

"The better you become at understanding what level of information is needed to evaluate and make a decision, and the better you become at zeroing in on that information and ensuring it is clear and accurate, the better you become at speeding up your process. As far as the questions go, let me show you the questions I ask myself each day."

With that, Marcus pulled out his notebook from his pocket once again and turned to a page in the very back. On the top Joey could see where he had written his list.[9]

DAILY QUESTIONS:

Personal Development
   What did I experience today that will help me become a better person? How can I continue to grow?

LDL
   What did I do today to develop leaders around me? What could I have done better?

---

9. Maxwell, John C. *How Successful People Think*. New York: Center Street, 2009.

Leadership

Did I follow the golden rule of leadership today? How do I know this?

Friends

Did I demonstrate love for my friends today?

Values

Did I live out the things I profess as important in my life today? What specific actions did I take or could I have taken to demonstrate my values to those around me?

Habits

Am I creating proper moral habits in my life? In what ways have I strayed from that which is right?

Learning

What did I learn today that I can use tomorrow?

Joey was astonished. "You ask yourself those questions every day?"

"Yes sir, 365 days a year!" Marcus responded. "But these are *my* questions. They aren't necessarily the right questions for you. We don't need Joey Cook asking the questions that will make him Marcus. We need Joey to be the best Joey he can be. In order to do that, you need to ask questions that are appropriate to your own values and goals as a leader."

"Man, it's no wonder you have mastered what it means to lead!" Joey exclaimed.

"If you spend every single day thinking about this stuff, you're bound to pick up something every now and then, but I haven't mastered anything. I've simply created habits that I believe lead to my own *eudaimonia* in life. I'm still learning every day what it means to lead authentically as Marcus!"

"So, how do I put this into action right now, today?" the young leader asked.

"Set aside time. Be intentional. Remove yourself from all the distractions of life and focus with the discipline worthy of your best effort and self.[10] Get a notebook, and keep it with you everywhere you go. And maybe most important of all, follow up your reflection with action!

"You can hear the greatest nugget of wisdom in the world. You can write it down and have the best intention for implementing it imaginable. But if you don't turn your reflection and thinking into action, what's the point? What's the point of having tremendous experiences if you aren't following those experiences up with reflection, critical thinking, and a plan of action for implementing changes to improve those experiences the next time they occur?

"You must be action-oriented while retaining a reflective posture. Reflection gives you confidence in who you are as a leader and decision-maker. It allows you to take both the good and the bad from each day and discover what to repeat and what to change. Reflection provides us with perspective on our experiences. Reflection takes our experiences and adds value."

"Okay, I think I'm picking up on all this, but I have one last question. What if the decision I have to make is time-critical? This is super helpful and all, but we have to figure this thing out by next week!" Joey said, a note of impatience in his voice.

"That's what the whole critical thinking and reflection process is about!" Marcus declared. "It's about speeding up your process by becoming a better thinker and reflector each and every day. An Air Force pilot by the name of John Boyd came up with the idea of the OODA Loop. Have you ever heard of it?"

"No, I don't think so."

"The OODA Loop was his way of making decisions faster

---

10. Ibid, Page 75.

than anyone else, and as a fighter pilot, being able to make quicker decisions than your opponent means you stay alive and in the fight longer. OODA stands for observe, orient, decide, and act.

"Observing and orienting is all about critical thinking. It's about taking in your surroundings, processing that information as quickly as possible, making a decision based on the information you have, and then choosing to act in accordance with that decision. Think about your time on the basketball court. The better you become at observing what's taking place around you, who's moving where, who's setting a screen, who's open for a pass, what defense the opposition is in, and what play you are running, the quicker you can orient yourself, make the right decision, and act in a way that puts your team at an advantage to score a basket.

"Leadership is the same way. The more time you spend refining your process, the more time you spend discerning what information is relevant and what isn't, the more time you spend reflecting on who you are becoming, the quicker you can orient yourself and make decisions, and the more confidence you can have in your authentic ability to lead in moments where time is a factor.

"We all would love the chance to have as much time as humanly possible to make every decision, but that just isn't practical. So you design your thinking process to prepare you to act in accordance with your values and standards in a timely manner. That can only happen when you have properly habituated what it means to be a person of introspection, a leader who is a thinker.

"Critical thinking in leadership is about so much more than just making the right decisions. You can be right all day long, but if you are ineffective at communicating those decisions in a way that everyone on your team can understand and implement, then it doesn't matter how right you are. You have to dig deeper into how you communicate that decision, the implications of the decision on everyone around you, and how your decision is perceived by everyone on your team.

"This is why reflecting every day on the smallest details of what you are doing and who you are becoming as a leader is so critical, because it is easy to feel as though you are approaching everything the right way and still not finding success, simply because you haven't become authentically aware of how your leadership decisions are being perceived by those around you.

"How do I get to this level of reflection?" Joey asked.

"You must become a leader of confident humility, Joey. That means you understand that your assumptions and the things you think you know could be wrong or distorted, but you are confident in the values and standards that are guiding you each and every day. You can only do that through proper reflection and critical thinking, but once you do, you can move beyond being a reactive leader, swayed to and fro by every little thing that happens to you. Instead you can become a leader who is proactive, thinking ahead of your opponents and your problems, taking charge of leading your followers each and every day.

"And once you have done that, maybe, just maybe, you can become a predictive leader, one who not only is proactive in who he and his team is becoming but one who can anticipate the challenges that lie ahead and prepare his team for those challenges in advance! When that occurs, you learn how to stay left of boom, avoiding the pitfalls and traps that come with the consequences of operating only with a reactive mindset."

And just like that, it dawned on Joey that he had the solution to his team's predicament. It wasn't something revolutionary. It was merely an extension of their values and the company's purpose applied to everyone within the organization. The thought of being a proactive and predictive leader had sparked an idea in him he hadn't considered before.

He grabbed the coin out of Marcus' hand before he could say anything else and gave it a toss.

They were back in the car.

Joey grabbed hold of the steering wheel again and turned around to tell his mentor about his revelation, but he was nowhere to be seen. He quickly pulled a U-turn and sped back to the office.

His assumptions about the way forward had been wrong all along, and he had Ron and Sam to thank for the discovery.

CHAPTER 11
Αγάπη
LOVE

"The best way to find yourself is to lose yourself in the service of others."

—MAHATMA GANDHI

JOEY KNEW THAT habituating a life of reflection would not necessarily yield moments of discovery every day, but as soon as Marcus had begun discussing being proactive and predictive instead of reactive, the young leader realized what his team had been missing all along.

They had worked for several months now on a business solution, a way to solve the technological challenges associated with their predicament. The world they operated in was shifting dramatically and rapidly away from the assembly line production floor they were accustomed to and into a world of automation. No longer would it be necessary to use human hands to create all their aircraft components. This shift, in what was being dubbed "Industry 4.0," meant that there would be fewer man-hours required for each piece they produced.

Industry 4.0 looked at the evolution that began with steam power, moved forward with electricity, took a mighty lead with computers, and was now in its fourth generation of significant advancement with artificial intelligence.[1] From a business mind-set, this was a necessity to keep pace with everyone else in the industry. Lower prices, lean processes, and efficiency in production were the name of the game.

Joey was proud of the work that his team had done to not only solve the problem at hand with their specific component but to take a forward-thinking viewpoint on how they could leverage technology such as additive manufacturing to ensure that the same problem wouldn't happen to them in the future.

Some of the components needed for older aircraft would still require the human element in their creation, but his R&D and QA teams had really leaned into a plan for how to quit being reactive and stop playing catch-up with their competitors. Instead, they would push for incorporating additive manufacturing into their series of upgrades; this would both increase efficiency and ensure that they could meet the standard of quality expected by Joey, and hopefully, in turn, the company as a whole.

This had everyone excited, but Joey knew it would be a hard sell because it would require the board to also establish a proactive and predictive mindset.

He hadn't classified it in those terms before Marcus explained it to him in Warren Buffett's office, but the business acumen and competency he had displayed while leading his team had helped push them toward the future anyway.

Joey was proud of his team for dreaming a bold dream with him in the last few weeks. They had now moved beyond their preconceived notions that this was just about finding a temporary solution and had taken the "long view" like Mr. Buffett.

This is absolutely in the sweet spot and worth swinging for the fences, Joey surmised to himself.

Without even knowing it, through a proper understanding of purpose, a big dream, a vision for what it could look like, and standards that were nonnegotiable in creating it, they had chal-

---

1. DePillis, Lydia. "GM Is Gone. Now Come 3D Printers and Robots." *CNN*, Cable News Network, 7 Mar. 2019, www.cnn.com/2019/03/07/economy/future-of-manufacturing-youngstown/index.html.

lenged their assumptions and emerged with a plan that would not only solve their problem, but also would move the company forward in ways they were not expecting.

What was different now, Joey realized, was that everything Marcus had explained about challenging his assumptions and using critical thinking as a leader went well beyond just the bottom line and future of manufacturing for his company.

The problem was they had come up with a business solution but still had a people issue. Just as he had been thinking about his inability to become a leader who develops other leaders, he realized that the human element of all of this would still make or break them in the end.

Sure, Joey had worked on belief and commitment, on discipline and ownership, and on resolve and reflection, but he had missed the heart of the problem to begin with. He and everyone else around him were still being reactive in how they thought about and led their people.

Joey realized that his assumptions about Sam and Ron were misguided. The young leader was still not content with their unwillingness to stick it out until the end, but he had not considered their point of view in all of this. The two of them came from the production floor and manufacturing side of the operation. Sam was one of the oldest employees in the entire company. Ron was in the middle of his career, and he had no idea how he was going to keep pace with all the changes that were coming.

The two men, hardened by everything going on around them, were fearful. It was not that they were necessarily unwilling to change, but everything they were being told about change made them retreat into a mode of self-preservation. They were scared that no one would go to bat for them, and lost in the shuffle of all of this change, they would be on the outside looking in when the dust settled.

Bill had done nothing but affirm their fears. Though Joey had been working hard to shift them away from purely extrinsic motivation to something much more meaningful and lasting, he couldn't really move the needle because their most basic human needs as men, providing for their families and giving them security, was being constantly threatened.

Bill used the fear of job loss and the idea that they were replaceable as bait to lure them away from Joey's team and back to their previous existence under his watch.

At first, Joey had been angry and disappointed. Now, he began to realize that he couldn't hope to convince them of his desire to see them achieve their own *eudaimonia* if he couldn't even provide them with the assurance of keeping their jobs.

He wanted what was best for them. He wanted them to live a life of *arete*. But without action, without demonstrating that desire to his team, what good was the blueprint for his vision and the plan forward for his company?

The young leader continued to reflect and process everything as he made his way back to the office. He turned on the lights to the twenty-third floor upon his arrival, broke out a fresh new notebook, and began to jot down his ideas for making sure everyone on his team felt valued in their role and secure in their future at the company.

He went back to everything Marcus had just described about reflection, trying to identify the daily questions that would guide him on his leadership quest. He then moved on to the critical thinking process. There was no doubting the purpose. He knew the question at hand.

He worked through the information he had available, trying to ensure it was clear and accurate, with enough depth and breadth to give him confidence in his decision-making. He began to make inferences about what could be done, while simultaneously working to challenge his assumptions and the implications of what he was considering. He tried to take in the points of view of everyone in the company, but he remained rooted in his desire to keep the purpose at the forefront of this decision.

After hours of wrestling with his thoughts, the young leader, already exhausted from the workweek and well into his Friday night, crafted a plan for how the company could move beyond the extrinsic motivators that kept them paralyzed with fear and uncertainty each day.

Just like President Lincoln, the purpose never wavered, but the vision for how to get there had moved beyond its original intent and shifted to include more than just meeting quarterly projections and providing the highest quality products possible. Quality, Joey now realized, was not just about the customer. "Providing what was needed to those who needed it when they needed it" was about every single member of their company.

Quality was for everyone!

Joey closed his notebook and checked his watch. It was 9:00 p.m., and he hadn't eaten a single thing since lunch. He headed back down to the lobby and walked out into the brisk Atlanta evening. He looked at the people, from every walk of life, and began to wonder about their stories. He wondered what life events had shaped their points of view. He pulled out his notebook and jotted a note to himself:

Work harder to see life the way others see it.

He wasn't sure what specific steps this would require, but he wanted to be more than merely a leader at work, caring for his followers Monday through Friday from nine to five. He wanted this to become an extension of who he was as a person.

It seemed as though everything Marcus had been teaching him was simply a part of who the old man was and how he lived his life. Developing other leaders just happened to be a natural outcome of his own *arete* and desire for *eudaimonia*.

Joey hailed an Uber and made his way over to one of his favorite restaurants in Little Five Points. If he was going to be here at this hour on a Friday, at least he could get some good food before heading home to crash.

He walked inside the local brewpub and made his way over to the bar. He sat down, breathed a huge sigh of exhaustion, and asked the bartender for a menu. While Joey looked for something to order and a cold beer to go with it, he heard Marcus' voice over the chatter of the patrons nearby.

"Anyone sitting here?" the familiar voice asked.

"No, it's all yours!" Joey responded, motioning toward the stool next to him. He pulled out his notebook with pride and showed Marcus the beginnings of his attempt to become an introspective leader. He apologized for snatching the coin from the old man's hand and the premature return from their last adventure. He shared the reasoning for that choice, explaining that he realized being proactive as a leader meant ensuring he met the needs of his people above all else.

He told Marcus how he wanted to accomplish the mission and thought they had a great plan for doing just that, but now he also knew how much he wanted to bring everyone along with him, to call them to be their best selves, and he didn't think he could do that if they were constantly worried about their jobs or just filling out the time sheet for a paycheck.

"The Mission, the Men, Me," he declared. He expected Marcus to pick up where they left off, offering advice or challenging him to think differently, but all the old man did was smile.

Instead they did something they hadn't had the chance to do at any point during Joey's leadership journey.

They just talked.

Marcus asked Joey about his upbringing, his parents, his schooling, where he gained his competitive streak, and how he became so good at basketball.

Joey heard stories from Marcus about his late wife, his kids, and his time flying in the Navy. The old man told "sea story" after "sea story," recalling the times in his life that had shaped him as a leader—times that would have been invisible to anyone who glanced at him in passing.

Before they knew it, they had been swapping stories for hours, the relationship between the mentor and mentee deepening with each encounter they recalled. They probably would have kept sharing, but the bartender, waiting patiently to find the right time, finally interrupted them and asked if they were done ordering for the night.

Marcus reached for his wallet. As he pulled out a credit card to pay for his bill, a coin fell out of his billfold and rolled onto the table in between the two men.

Joey picked it up and looked it over. This one had a picture of a lion, with the word αγάπη below.

He looked at his watch and noticed that it was after midnight.

"Wow, we've been chatting for over three hours," he said to the old man.

"Yeah. It's amazing what it does for the soul, am I right?" Marcus replied.

"You know what that means?" Joey responded. "It's a new day. You can show me what this coin has to offer!"

Marcus looked at Joey with a glance of uncertainty.

"I've been saving this coin for weeks now, waiting for the right moment to share it with you," the old man said. "It's important to know, though, that everyone's leadership journey is different. We all begin in a different place, with different experiences, and different habits already formed in our lives. At **LDL**, we always hope our members will continue to progress, but it's never a guarantee. Some people are recommended but refuse to begin the process in the first place.

"I knew early on with you that we would get there, but this coin is the pinnacle of our journey together, son. You have to arrive at this place on your own. It has to be something that you discover for yourself. *You* have to fully embrace what it means to lead."

Joey looked at Marcus, thinking that even though the calendar had turned to Saturday, the old man would still refuse to take him on the next adventure, that he was still unprepared for the next challenge before him.

He looked down at the countertop at the coin again and was elated when he heard the old man's soft voice simply say, "You're ready."

Joey didn't look up. He reached for the coin and picked it up. He knew deep down this would be the final toss he made before he met with the board. Everything he had been building toward as a leader came down to this. He flung the coin in the air, squinting his eyes as the flash of light dissipated and rain began to fall steadily on him.

Joey scanned the horizon through the falling raindrops. He looked around at the marble stones lined in perfect rows and knew exactly where they were: Arlington National Cemetery.

The young leader had never visited the site where so many brave men and women were buried, but he sensed immediately the raw power and emotion that emerged simply by standing firmly on such sacred ground. He looked ahead through the steady rain and saw a pair of headstones in front of him. He turned around to ask Marcus if this is what he was supposed to see, but the old man was nowhere to be found.

It was only fitting, Joey thought, *that this last journey, much like the one he took to the South Pacific, was his and his alone.*

Marcus had given him so much over the last few months, but this was clearly intended to be a moment of solitude, a period of reflection for the young leader. As time momentarily stood still, Joey looked across the thousands upon thousands of other headstones that lined the rows at Arlington.

He didn't know their stories, but he wanted to. He wanted to know them all.

He thought about how what they were willing to do, what

they gave up, wasn't merely a marker of tremendous leadership or bravery or service or sacrifice. It wasn't about one singular piece of them. It was about all of them.

Joey looked back down and focused on the two headstones in front of him. He wondered why he hadn't been sent to witness their actions. Why hadn't he been brought to their funerals, to watch their friends and family and country pay their respects? He wondered why this moment, by himself, was the pinnacle moment of his leadership journey.

He moved forward, ever so slowly, and knelt down. He took notice of the two stones, different only in their inscriptions from the thousands of others that stretched from his right to his left, and read the one on the right out loud:

Brendan
Looney
LT US Navy
Feb 24 1981
Sep 21 2010
Operation
Enduring
Freedom
U.S. Navy Seal
Loving Husband
Son & Brother

Joey looked to his left and read the second one:

> Travis L
> Manion
> 1st LT USMC
> Nov 19 1980
> Apr 29 2007
> Iraqi Freedom
> Silver Star
> Bronze Star W/V
> Purple Heart
> If Not Me
> Then Who

He didn't know these two men, and he didn't have to. Just by being there, in the presence of their final resting place, he knew what they had sacrificed, what they had given for their country and for those around them.

But at the same time, he wanted to know their stories. He wanted to learn from their example. What could they teach him about who he was trying to become?

His eyes were still glued to the second marker, fixated on the words at the bottom that stared back at him, piercing through to his soul.

IF NOT ME

THEN WHO

If not me, then who? Joey closed his eyes, repeating the phrase over and over to himself as he reached in his pocket and grabbed the coin. He opened his eyes and found himself back on the stool at the bar.

The bartender looked his way and told him it was closing time. Joey reached for his wallet, but the man behind the counter told him not to worry, his friend had covered his tab.

As Joey stood up to walk toward the door, the bartender called him back over. He pulled a piece of paper from his back pocket and handed it to Joey. "Your friend left this behind as well," he said. "Told me to give it to you before you left."

Joey grabbed the paper from the bartender and thanked him. He called for an Uber and then walked out into the cool night air and noticed that a steady rain had started falling here as well.

He hopped in the car and began the ride back to the office. He pulled out the paper, which turned out to be a letter, and began to read:

Joey,

I've been holding onto this note for some time now.

I want you to know, first and foremost, that I'm proud of you.

I'm proud of your journey and I'm proud of how hard you have worked and continue to work to become your best self, to reach your own eudaimonia in life.

I promised you several weeks ago that I would share with you the **LDL** *pyramid.*

Joey flipped the page over and saw Marcus' drawing below:

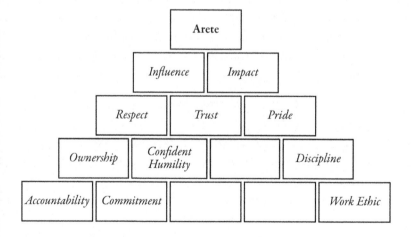

He saw many of the words he had been accustomed to hearing over the last few months: accountability, commitment, discipline, ownership, humility, and of course, at the very top, arete.

"Sustained excellence," he told himself, as the driver turned around and gave him an awkward glance.

"Sorry!" Joey said to the man, as he looked back down.

It was strange, he thought, that the pyramid was incomplete, with three blocks still empty stacked together at the bottom.

He turned back to the first page and continued reading.

> *No doubt you have seen the empty spaces below. It's time to fill in the rest of the pyramid for you.*
>
> *Travis Manion and Brendan Looney were roommates together at the Naval Academy. They were best friends, but they were fiercely competitive with each other. Each of them wanted to make the other one better, to push each other as hard as possible because they knew what most likely awaited them after graduation. Both of them knew that the United States was at war. They knew that in the fields in which they hoped to enter, that combat was inevitable.*
>
> *Travis was a nationally ranked wrestler and Brendan was a tremendous athlete and lacrosse player. They used their experiences on the mat and the fields of friendly strife to prepare them for who they were becoming as men.*
>
> *Travis and Brendan understood what it means to call each other up to our own standard of excellence in life. They understood what it means to be a leader who develops other leaders. Travis and Brendan understood what it means to love.*

Joey flipped the page back over and noticed that one of the words on the bottom had just been filled in.

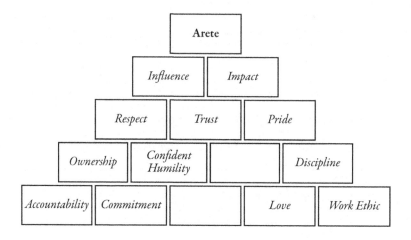

"The old man is up to his tricks again," Joey murmured to himself.

I know love isn't what anyone expects when we talk about warriors and leaders, but it's absolutely critical to becoming someone worth following, someone who has the influence and impact necessary to reach a life of **arete**.

When Coach Swinney finally saw his level of belief translate into reaching the mountaintop and winning the National Championship, it wasn't because he preached effort, determination, resiliency, focus, or discipline.

He expected those things to be factors in their outcome, but the process to get there was centered around one word: love.

He told a reporter after the game, "The difference in the game was love. I told them, tonight we are going to win, and it is because we love each other."[2]

That's what he told his team, and that's what he reflected on in the first moments after victory was finally achieved.

His belief was founded in love!

In the end, your ability to love may be the single greatest factor in your ability to lead.

Love is meeting the needs of others ahead of your own.

Love is seeking the highest good of your team.

And just like all of the things we have discussed, love requires you to act.

Love is something you do!

Love is not passive.

Love is not just some feeling.

Love is a decision you make!

Love is a choice, Joey!

Meeting the needs of others through the actions you take is what this whole leadership journey is about.

The Mission, the Men, Me is nothing more than a representation of your love.

Love is complex. The Greeks had six words for it, for goodness sake. Philia, or brotherly love, was exhibited between these two friends, and become a part of their identity in who they were as Navy and Marine Corps officers. They had each other's backs. They were loyal. Not only loyal to each other in the present moment, but loyal to each other's future best self.

---

2. Chambers, Brandon. "Dabo Swinney's Message to His Team-LOVE." Online Video Clip. YouTube. 10 Jan 2017.

Brendan's life motto was "Be strong. Be accountable. Never complain."[3] He and Travis embodied that for each other and for everyone else around them. This was their standard, the code they lived by.

You see, loyalty to your team isn't about blindly looking out for them in a way that shields them from failure. Loyalty to your team says that you know what they are capable of becoming, and you will do everything in your power to help them get there, including holding them to the standards that will be necessary to accomplish the mission.

Loyalty is a true, willing, and unfailing devotion. It means eliminating your own personal interests so the common cause you are fighting for can triumph.

Love is the same way. **Philia,** *brotherly love, is forged through common experiences and teaches us to meet the needs of others ahead of our own because we know they will do the same for us. This type of love is built out of mutual respect and trust.*

Joey thought back to that Sunday in the office. His team had come and helped him prepare with that same mentality and mindset.

The other type of love I want to share with you is **agape.**

Agape *is unconditional, sacrificial love. It says that regardless of whether or not we have shared experiences, regardless of whether you have wronged me, regardless of whether you deserve it, or regardless of if you will show*

---

3. "Meet Brendan." *The Brendan Looney Foundation.*
   https://www.brendanlooneyfoundation.org/meet-brendan/

*me love back, I **still** choose to put your needs ahead of my own.*

This is what it means to lead.

It means that people will wrong you. It means that people will put their own interests ahead of yours. It means that not everyone will believe in your vision and the standards required to get there.

And it means that even when those things happen, you will continue to love and call others to be their best selves. You will continue to put their needs ahead of your own.

*Leadership is a complex process, just like love, but it's also really simple. In the end, **leadership is love**, and just like all the other traits we have been working on habituating, it manifests itself through the actions you take that demonstrate that love.*

Service, even if it is not reciprocated, and sacrifice, even if there is a personal risk, are merely the indications to everyone around you that you love them.

Service, Joey, is the demonstration of your love!

The young leader turned the letter over one more time to see that another of the boxes had been filled in with the word *service*.

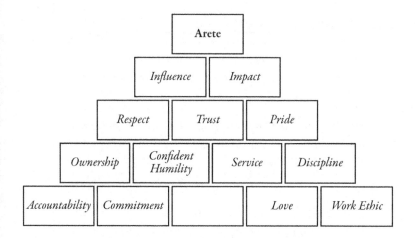

Travis Manion and Brendan Looney were full of love for their fellow Marines and SEALs. They were full of love for their country. They were full of love for their families and friends. They were full of love for each other.

That love, the type of love that earned them respect and trust from everyone they had the chance to lead and interact with, was demonstrated through the ways they served others and their willingness to sacrifice their own needs for the needs of everyone else.

They both paid the ultimate sacrifice because of that love.

And they were prepared for that sacrifice, not because in some grand moment, the hero inside of them rose up and took on the challenge they faced. No, they were prepared for those moments because they had properly habituated the daily actions necessary so that when the big moment arrived, those actions were a natural extension of who they already had become.

They were heroes because of their habits.

They lived "If not me, then who" every single day.

Those five words, uttered by Travis before going on his second deployment to Iraq in which he was killed by a sniper while trying to help two of his wounded Marines get to safety, are the embodiment of what it means to step out and lead.[4]

We don't choose to serve and sacrifice for others because we have to or because someone told us we needed to do so in order to lead them. We serve and sacrifice for others because we love them and we can't help but serve them.

It's time for you to fully understand what it means to lead. It's time for you to put the needs of your team ahead of your own.

It's time for you to LOVE!

After all, if you won't do it, then who will?

Your Friend,
Marcus

As Joey finished reading Marcus' letter, he turned the page over one more time to see the **LDL** pyramid that would help guide him towards excellence in his own life.

The young leader noticed that there was still one spot left empty. Dead center, at the bottom of the pyramid, he was still missing one key ingredient to understanding how to live a life of *arete*.

He looked back at the note one more time, anticipating that something else would magically appear, but nothing changed.

---

4. Sileo, Tom, and Manion, Tom. *Brothers Forever*. Boston: Da Capo Press, 2014.

Joey folded the letter and put it in his pocket.

He thought about the words Marcus had written and what he had observed in Arlington National Cemetery.

He thought about Travis and Brendan.

He thought about his team.

He thought about what serving them was going to require.

He thought about what he would potentially have to sacrifice by loving them.

Then he thought once more about those five words.

"If not me, then who?"

CHAPTER 12

Χαρακτήρ
CHARACTER

"From self-knowledge comes character and integrity, and from character and integrity comes leadership."

—VINCE LOMBARDI

J OEY CLOSED THE door to the boardroom and walked over to a seat in the company's elegant twenty-fifth-floor waiting room. He took a deep breath, closed his eyes, and began to replay the last week in his mind.

His team had done what they set out to do. Up against what appeared to be an impossible deadline just two weeks ago, they had come up with a clear way forward for the company, not just in the production of one individual component, but in how they could approach the future as a whole.

After getting back to the office on Monday morning a week ago, Joey shared his plan for keeping "quality" at the forefront of how the company developed their own employees as well.

Most of his team seemed shocked at the ideas he presented. They were not surprised that he would come up with a solution to solve their problem, but they were stunned that he did so in a way that included their growth and development with the company as well. He had put their needs in front of his own, and they all knew it was a longshot to ever get the board to sign off on his plan.

This was going to require a commitment from the board unlike any they had ever undertaken. It would mean both a financial commitment and a significant time commitment. It also would mean that they would no longer treat everyone as expendable. They would have to invest in their people above all else.

After running through his ideas and leaving the team to crunch the numbers and come up with a proposal for what this would look like, Joey set off for the manufacturing facility a few miles up the road.

The young leader walked in and found Sam and Ron hard at work. The two men who had been the most difficult to deal with and who had left the team hanging just twelve days before their deadline were laboring away in their regular, everyday jobs.

Joey went up to each of them and apologized for the position he had put them in. He apologized for the way they must have felt and how fearful they must still be about the future of their employment. He apologized for the way the company had treated them, and he promised that even though he could not guarantee a change in the organization's approach, he was going to lay it all on the line for them when he presented his solution to the board.

Joey thanked each of them for the role they played in helping him discover his true purpose and gave them each a big hug. He then looked each of them in the eye and uttered three words they probably had never heard before at work: "I love you!"

They might think he was crazy and officially off his rocker, but the young leader didn't care. What was even more important, he thought, was his determination to not just tell them he cared for them, but to show them and everyone else on his team each and every day what they meant to him.

Joey then walked over to Bill and finally confronted the man who had given his team so much grief over the last few months.

"Hey, I don't know why you've had it out for me and my team from the start, and I also don't know why you felt that you had to put Ron and Sam in a position to choose between our team and the future of their jobs, but I want to let you know that what you are doing here is the wrong approach. We need to be calling each and every one of our employees to be the best versions of themselves. We should be lifting them up, not pinning them down with fear and intimidation.

"Here's the thing. You can continue to come after me all you want. You can call me out for the failures I've had the last few weeks. And you can do everything in your power to force me out of my leadership role in the future. But you're done coming after my team. They have done nothing but demonstrate a standard of excellence in the way they've worked the past few months. They have exemplified everything I wanted them to do, and they have been the catalyst behind everything that we are going to present to the board next week. If this company changes for the better, you will only have them to thank!"

Bill had not responded very well, but Joey stood his ground and tried his hardest to convince the senior executive that the way forward needed to be different. He remembered Marcus' words about the golden rule of leadership, and even though Sam and Ron probably would never hear about this interaction, he wanted to make sure he was following the way he wanted to be followed.

It was to no avail, however. The VP berated the young leader for daring to speak up. He promised him that he was nearing the end of his time in a leadership position and he should just enjoy it while it lasted.

Joey took out his notebook and began to jot down some thoughts, much to Bill's chagrin. He realized that he might have come on too strong and perhaps it hadn't been the best way to interact with the senior executive after all. He would look at this later in the day when he reflected on the work he still had to do to become the type of leader he was capable of becoming.

Joey's thoughts drifted back to the present as he sat on the chair outside of the boardroom.

He thought about the last hour. It had not been the same disaster as two weeks ago. He had grown and was much more prepared and confident to present his ideas in an authentic way that represented his belief about the future of the company.

He told the board members that it was going to require a serious investment of resources to make it a reality. They were not going to hit their quarterly projections. But they would make up for it the next quarter, and six months from now, they would be not only meeting their quotas but doing so while being predictive about the future of their industry and organization.

No longer would they have to react to the changes occurring all around them. They would lead the charge and provide a product of greater quality that was significantly cheaper, all while supporting the growth and development of their employees to become proactive and predictive in their own careers.

Of course, there was significant skepticism. Bill led the charge to try and tear down everything he suggested.

This time, Greg remained silent, allowing the young leader to stand his ground and defend the position he had spent the last two weeks thinking about in depth.

As the board sat there deliberating, Joey wasn't sure what the end result would be, but it didn't really matter. He had laid it all on the line for his team, and there was a good chance that his proposal would not only be rejected, but that he had put himself in an unrecoverable position with the company moving forward.

No matter, he thought. *In the end, this was the right thing to do.*

"If not me, then who?" As Joey uttered those words quietly, a hand grabbed him by the shoulder. Greg sat down next to him and looked him in the eyes.

"I like that!" the COO said. "What are you, some kind of slogan generator?"

Joey found it odd that the senior executive would use the same language Marcus had used in their first encounter, but he dismissed the coincidence.

"Hey, thank you for having my back the past few months," he told the COO. "It seemed at times that you were the only one who believed I could lead this team."

"That's what we do," Greg replied. "We identify potential and call people up to the excellence they are capable of."

Joey realized this could no longer be considered a coincidence, but before he could say another word, Greg popped open his briefcase to reveal a group of shiny old coins.

"Wait, you're **LDL** too?" Joey shouted.

"Of course. Who do you think slipped that coin in your pocket at the last board meeting?" Greg responded.

"It was you! You gave me the Rowling coin! You sent me on a journey of discovery about what it really means to fail!" Joey couldn't believe it.

"I told Marcus that you were exactly the type of leader we needed in this role, and I asked him if he could help guide you along the way," Greg said.

"Leaders developing leaders. So you orchestrated this whole thing?"

"I guess you could say that. But that's what we do, Joey. We learn what it means to lead and then we pass that knowledge on to other leaders. What good is all of this if we just keep it to ourselves? Marcus helped me earn my coin, and I knew he would be the perfect person to help you in your journey as well. You should consider yourself lucky too. The old man is a legend!"

Joey looked down at the briefcase in front of him. Greg had nowhere near the number of coins as Marcus, but they were still just as exquisite as the ones the old man had shared time and time again over the last few months.

Joey began to pull them out, one by one, looking Greg's way as the COO told him about the journeys connected to each one.

A coin with a bridge on the front. Joey thought it must have represented the same bridge Marcus had shared with him on his first journey.

"Dr. Martin Luther King, Jr. Courage."

Then there was one with a baseball bat and a Brooklyn Dodgers cap. Joey knew what this one had to be.

"Jackie Robinson?" he asked Greg.

"Ahh, good guess. Branch Rickey actually."

"Here's Jackie's!" Joey pulled out the coin to see the number 42 engraved. He saw another one with boxing gloves, similar to President Roosevelt's.

"Joe Louis!" Greg said emphatically. "What a tremendous story of perseverance in the face of adversity!"

Joey saw one with a University of Tennessee block T. "Man, I can't catch a break with all of these stories about my team's rivals. Let me guess, Pat Summitt?"

"Right you are! What an incredible example of ownership and inspiration."

Then the senior executive got serious for a moment. "Joey, I want to tell you something important. Everyone's leadership journey is different. And everyone's leadership journey requires an understanding of the moral exemplars that will have the biggest influence on their own individual path to a life of *arete*.

"Just because Marcus only had time to share several very specific stories of great leaders with you doesn't mean that the world isn't full of other people who have habituated a life of excellence and are worthy of studying. Each of these individuals has something they can teach us. They've all earned their coins. I challenge you to expand your horizons and look at people from every background and walk of life who can show you what it means to be a leader worth following. Only when you do this will you have the understanding necessary to be prepared to help the leaders you are developing. You can't know what's best for the people you lead unless you are continuing to learn and grow yourself."

Joey nodded. Then he looked back at the briefcase and picked up another coin.

This one seemed a little bit shinier than the rest.

He looked down and saw an aircraft on the front.

Χαρακτήρ was written below the plane.

"Another pilot!" Joey exclaimed as he looked at the inscription below. "Whose coin is this?"

The COO paused for a brief second.

"It's yours," Greg said softly.

"Mine? What do you mean?"

"You have earned your coin, Joey. And as the person who nominated you for the **LDL** journey, I'm the one who gets to present it to you."

"I don't understand. How did I possibly earn my coin? I haven't done anything like the men and women I've seen in the coins Marcus shared with me," Joey said.

"Earning your coin isn't always about some grand moment," Greg answered. "Remember, this whole thing is simply about developing proper habits. And proper habits lead to moments in our lives that represent and showcase the fact that we have embodied the traits we so desperately desire to incorporate.

"For some people, this may require exemplifying those values in a way that couldn't be reasonably expected of another person in their situation. But for others, it's just a simple interaction that indicates to everyone around you that those values have taken hold in your life. You earned your coin in that Boardroom in there just now," Greg said, pointing to the door. "You showcased incredible leadership to everyone in that room."

Greg flipped the coin, and Joey found himself just one hour before, standing in front of the board and presenting his case.

He didn't really think he was doing anything exceptional. All he was doing was putting into practice everything Marcus had taught him.

He watched himself explain the solution to the predicament they found themselves in. He told the board that downsizing would be inevitable, and he understood that. But there were certain legacy parts, just like the one he and his team had been working on, that would need more care and attention.

Perhaps if they allowed the older generation of workers like Sam to continue producing the components that still needed human attention and would not be able to be produced at this point through additive manufacturing, they could preserve the work of men and women that had given decades to their company long enough to get them to retirement.

He explained that the middle generation of employees, men and women like Ron who had been working for a while but were not even close to retirement age, would need to be retrained and receive proper certification in order to operate the machinery for the new additive manufacturing process. This would require specialized schooling, but it was worth the investment to keep good people employed and progressing in their careers.

"If we are going to move forward and be proactive and predictive with our technology, we should do the same for our people," the young leader proclaimed. He then outlined the need for a young generation of workers who were entering the workforce already prepared for the tasks at hand.

This would require less man-hours per part produced, but the skills they could bring to the table would be in high-demand, and therefore, the company would have to stand out from the rest in order to attract them. All of this, Joey said, would create a flexible manufacturing base that could adapt to customers' needs quickly and would also allow them to pivot to other markets as necessary.

Joey shared how he believed in his heart that if they invested in their people, the company would grow to heights it had not imagined previously. And if they did it all with a focus on quality for everyone that ever came in contact with their products, they would stand out in a crowded market.

"We can no longer operate out of fear, with everyone holding on to as much corporate knowledge as possible, never willing to share or develop anyone else for concern that they might lose their job if they help serve others."

Bill jumped in and continued to blame Joey for the problems at hand. He balked at the price tag associated with Joey's "solution" and recommended that not only should the plan not be implemented, but members of Joey's team should be let go or reprimanded for even suggesting such a preposterous idea.

The young leader didn't blink. He looked right at Bill, then looked at the rest of the board. "I'm afraid if that's your choice, then you'll have to let me go too. I'm not going to work for a company that puts its profits ahead of its people!"

With that, Greg flipped the coin and the two of them emerged back on the bench outside the conference room.

"You see, Joey, you proved in that moment that you had learned what it means to lead. Without even thinking, you were willing to sacrifice your future at this company for the sake of your team. You put them first, making sure it was apparent to the board that they were responsible for any and all of your successes and that when this plan was put in place, the future progress and advancement of the company would be because of the work they did. You made a choice. And that choice demonstrated what we knew about you all along."

"I didn't even really consider another option," Joey said.

"I know, and that's why this coin is now yours," Greg responded, handing the shiny new object to the young man.

"All of this, Joey, every single thing you have learned about yourself and what it means to lead, comes down to one simple concept: character. The Greek word for *character* means 'the engraving of a coin.' That's why we use these to create our journeys," Greg said, pointing to the object in Joey's hand. "When a coin is engraved, you take something that has form and shape, and you imprint on it markings that identify to everyone else what its value is.

"Your character is the same way. Your character indicates to the rest of the world what your value is. The actions you take tell everyone around you who you are and what you are worth. Habits are consistent actions, and your character is nothing more than the sum of all of your moral habits, the consistent actions you take daily that indicate to everyone what you stand for. And character cannot be faked. Sure, it can be fabricated for a little while, but eventually, when the choice must be made between looking out for yourself and serving others, your true identity will be revealed.

"Theodore Roosevelt said that 'bodily vigor is good, and vigor of intellect is even better, but far above both is character. It is true, of course, that a genius may, on certain lines, do more than a brave man who is not a genius; and so, in sports, vast physical strength may overcome weakness, even though the body may have in it the heart of a lion. But, in the long run, in the great battle of life, no brilliancy of intellect, no perfection of bodily development, will count when weighed in the balance against the assemblage of virtues, active and passive, of moral qualities, which we group together under the name of character; and if between any two contestants, even in sport or work, the difference in character on the right side is as great as the difference of intellect or strength the other way, it is the character side that will always win.'[1]

"All of it matters, Joey. Every single quality you have been working to develop. Each journey you have undertaken. It is all a part of becoming who you were meant to be. Becoming a leader worth following starts with an intentional effort, day in and day out, to demonstrate proper habits of character. It is just modest improvement, consistently done. Do you have the letter Marcus left you at the bar last week?"

---

1. Roosevelt, Theodore. "Character and Success." *The Outlook,* 31 Mar. 1900, www.foundationsmag.com/tr-character.html

"Yeah, it's right here," Joey said, pulling it out of his jacket pocket, wondering how Greg possibly could have known about it. They looked at the pyramid together.

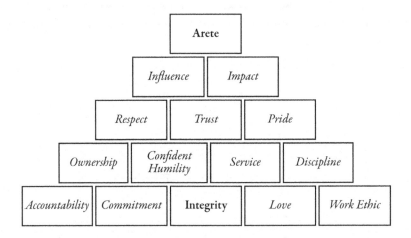

At the bottom, Joey could see the final word filled in for him: INTEGRITY.

"Integrity is the consistent alignment of your actions with the values and standards you have committed yourself to," Greg said. "*Integrity*, from the same word we use for *integer*, a whole number, means that you are complete and whole, undivided regardless of circumstances. Being whole as a person means that the values and standards you have professed as important in your life are consistently lived out through the actions you take. Integrity means that the sum of your habits, that character you are working so hard to develop, all of those collective little pieces, are equal to *one*, a whole number. Integrity is the cornerstone of leadership, son."

Joey looked at the pyramid. It all made sense to him in this moment. Everything Marcus had been preaching was not really about leadership after all. It was about his character and his ability to consistently live a life in accordance with his values, striving to be a person of integrity each and every day.

"It seems like a pretty lofty goal," he said to Greg.

"It is. And that's why perfection isn't the standard. Best is the standard! You will never get there, but you must work with the effort necessary each day to get a little bit closer, to become a little more whole in your journey to live a life of *arete* and achieve your own *eudaimonia*."

Joey looked back down at the pyramid below.

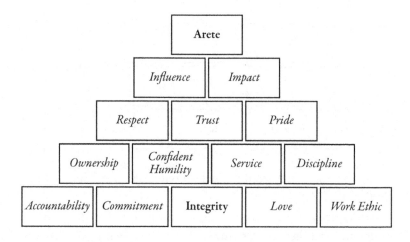

"It all works together upwards toward that life of sustained excellence," Greg said. "When you are committed to accountability, you take ownership of everything you are responsible for. When you are committed to a life of integrity, you can have confident humility in who you are as a leader. When you are a person striving for integrity and you do so with a habit of love, you can't help but serve others. When you combine love with a strong work ethic, you will pursue a disciplined life. When you are a person who fully embraces ownership and you present an attitude of confident humility as a leader, you earn the respect of those around you. When you combine confident humility with a life of service, you gain trust. A disciplined pursuit of the right things with service at the forefront leads to pride in the work you do. Trust is the currency of leadership, and when you combine respect and trust, which is earned and not given, you become a person of influence.

"Leadership, at the end of the day, is nothing more than a relationship of influence, founded on a life focused on the pursuit of integrity. When you have the trust of everyone around you and everyone can take pride in the work you do, you prepare yourself for a life of impact. And when you combine influence as a leader with impact, well, then you have arrived at a life of sustained excellence, you have achieved your own version of *arete*."

The idea that all of these concepts individually work together to reach the top, starting with striving to live a life of integrity, was what Marcus was trying to teach him all along.

"This is amazing!" Joey said. "But how do I build this in my team? How do I take the individual lessons and make them something we pursue together?"

"That's the challenge of being a leader, Greg answered. "You can't get there until you realize what it's going to take individually. But once you realize that, you now must pursue 'collective character' within your team. Your team's collective character is its culture, the sum of all of the individual habits that you form as a team that show the rest of the world what your value is as an organization.

"And guess what? Your team just got bigger," the COO said, much to Joey's surprise.

"Bigger? After that?"

"Yes sir. The board has agreed to adopt your proposal, and they want you to oversee its implementation. Congratulations, son. You are now the new vice president of manufacturing here!"

Joey looked back at the pyramid. Then he pulled out the napkin Marcus gave him several months back.

He looked at the bridge.

He looked at the pyramid again.

He looked at *his* coin.

Then he looked up to ask Greg one more question, but the COO was nowhere to be found.

"Man, I've got to get one of them to teach me how to do that," the young leader said as he put the coin in his pocket and made his way to the elevator.

As he walked into the twenty-third-floor conference room, everyone began to cheer wildly. Time stood still for Joey as he thought about everything he had experienced since he met that old man on the bench.

He thought about all of the incredible stories he had been able to witness.

He thought about how much he had learned as a leader in just a few short months.

He thought about what was in front of him and his team.

He knew it wasn't going to be easy.

After all, leadership was proving to be exhausting.

But none of that mattered right now.

What mattered now were the people surrounding him in that room, the joy on their faces at having accomplished something special together permanently etched in his brain.

He felt the coin once more in his pocket just to make sure this wasn't some kind of dream.

Nope. This was real.

The young leader was now officially a member of the **LDL** team.

EPILOGUE

"[Character] is the fuel that allows common people to produce uncommon results."

—ANDREW CARNEGIE

J OEY WALKED OUT of the boardroom, the door from the lavish twenty-fifth-floor corner office closing behind him. He was trying to process what he had just been told, what the news meant for him and his future at the Fortune 500 company where he found himself employed.

He walked past his corner office to the elevator and stood there, forgetting to press the button to travel to the lobby below.

Eventually, Greg, the company's chief executive officer, approached, pressing the button Joey had forgotten, and asking his closest friend and colleague if he was all right.

"Congrats, man. Everyone is rooting for you. We know you have what it takes to lead this organization. We wouldn't have chosen you for the job if we didn't. Just make sure you try and remember that in the coming weeks when things get tough!"

Joey gave his mentor and friend a big hug, in no way trying to make light of the moment.

None of this was about him, after all, and it had not been for the past five years. Everything he had achieved, and everything the company would continue to achieve, was because of the tremendous people he worked with.

Joey left the building and walked outside into the bright

morning sunlight. He headed down Baker Street and walked the three blocks to Centennial Olympic Park.

Joey glanced up from the trail and noticed an older gentleman sitting on a bench off to the side of the path, dressed in a tattered sport coat and jeans, a pair of loafers on his feet.

The same man who had changed everything about Joey's life five years ago was sitting there, waiting for him to arrive.

"Marcus! How have you been, old friend?"

"It's another beautiful morning, and hey, I hear there was some big news coming out of the glass palace today!"

"Yeah, it's crazy to think that five years ago I was named VP of manufacturing. Then when Greg took over as CEO, he named me as his COO, and now that he is retiring to join the **LDL** Council full-time, the company has decided to name me as his replacement."

"At only thirty-six years old, no less!" the old man responded.

"Marcus, you know as well as I do how little that matters to me."

"I know, but it's still an impressive accomplishment."

"No, what's impressive has been the transformation of this company in just a few short years. To go from a regional producer of aircraft parts to one of the most technologically advanced man-ufacturers in the country...man, we really have a strong team here. And, we were just named one of the top ten places to work in the Southeast. It's incredible what can happen when a group of people believe in each other, serve each other, and are united in common purpose and direction for where they want to be and what they want to accomplish. When I was named VP, I thought maybe I finally had this leadership thing wired. Turns out, I keep learning something new from my team every single day."

"Well, congrats, my friend. I'm proud of you and I love you."

"I love you too, old man!" Joey replied. "And don't let Greg get too comfortable. I'm working as hard as I possibly can to help enough people earn their coins to join the **LDL** Council myself. That's the real goal. All this other stuff, all the accolades, they're nice and I'm appreciative of what they stand for and represent. But most of all I'm proud of the people that we get to help become their best selves.

"Leaders Developing Leaders. That's who we are. And we are always looking for the next group of people who want to join us on this incredible adventure to discover what it means to live a life of *arete* each and every day!"

GLOSSARY OF TERMS

Συνάντηση
A meeting or encounter

Εὐδαιμονία
Eudaimonia is a Greek word used to describe the highest form of "human flourishing." The word literally means "good spirit" and was used by Aristotle to describe the highest human good one can achieve.

Πιστεύω
To believe in something, to trust

δέσμευση
Commitment

Κίνητρο
Motivation

Παιδεία
Paideia is a word used to describe the holistic education of the ideal Greek citizen. This included intellectual, moral, and physical refinement and a focus on the things that are beautiful and good. It is tied closely to the idea of arete. One of the best representations of paideia is from Plato's Republic when he says that "the hard is the good."[1]

Αρετή

Arete means excellence of any kind. The term is closely akin to moral virtue, that which is always good. Arete is deeply connected with the notion of the fulfillment of purpose or the act of living up to one's full potential in life.

Αμαρτία

To miss the mark, fall short of an objective

Ιδιοκτησία

To take ownership of something

ελαστικότητα

Resilience, elasticity

σκέψη

Thinking, thought, reflection, meditation

αγάπη

Sacrificial, universal, and unconditional love that persists regardless of circumstance

χαρακτήρ

Character, an engraved mark like the markings on a coin, a symbol or imprint on the soul

---

1. Plato. *Plato's The Republic.* New York: Books, Inc., 1943. Print.

ABOUT THE AUTHOR

ORIGINALLY FROM GEORGETOWN, South Carolina, Justin Mears is a 2009 graduate of the United States Naval Academy and a 2016 graduate of Georgetown University. After completing flight school and earning his "wings of gold" as a naval aviator, Justin's first assignment was to Helicopter Sea Combat Squadron Twenty-Six in Norfolk, Virginia. He deployed twice to the Middle East with HSC-26 Detachment One, and after completing his first tour, he returned to his alma mater. At the Naval Academy, he served as a senior instructor in the Leadership, Ethics, and Law Department, teaching undergraduate courses in leadership and character development and serving as the deputy director for the Center for Experiential Leadership Development. After transitioning from active duty, Justin founded Lead-Off, an experiential leadership and character development consultancy based out of Greenville, South Carolina. LeadOff works with a range of organizations, including business, government, military, and athletic departments, as Justin and his team strive to develop leaders of character who operate with a non-negotiable standard of excellence in every area of their lives. He is married to his wife of ten years, Candice, who is also a 2009 Naval Academy graduate, former aviator, and Navy veteran. They have a four-year-old son, Jackson.

ACKNOWLEDGMENTS

To Candice, thank you for putting up with my crazy writing process. I know I spent days and weeks in a daze, lost in my thoughts as I tried to piece together this book into something you would be proud of.

To my friends, thank you for letting me bounce ideas off of you and for indulging my requests to read chapter after chapter for me for months on end.

To my family, thank you for encouraging me to put pen to paper and for continuing to help me believe throughout the entire process that the end result would be worth it.

And most importantly, to my dad, thank you for the endless support, the hours and hours of conversation from the very beginning about my dream for this book down to the smallest detail about where *The Coin* was headed, whose journeys should be told, and all the research you did behind the scenes so I could focus on the story itself. Your support and vision for where this is headed keeps my bridge CAVU.

Did you enjoy this book? Then please consider sharing it with others!

- Share or mention the book on your social media platforms, using the hashtags #TheCoin and #LeadersDevelopingLeaders
- Write a book review on Amazon so that we can continue to spread the message of LDL!
- Pick up a copy for friends, family, or even strangers-we believe that this is a message that will challenge anyone who reads it to work towards becoming a better version of themselves.
- Share this message on Twitter, Facebook, or Instagram: I loved #TheCoin by @jmears26
- Follow along with the work we are doing at LeadOff by visiting our site https://www.leadoffllc.com and signing up to receive updates on the LDL movement!

I am always open and available to talk leadership and character development with anyone and everyone. Do not hesitate to reach out if there is anything I can do to help you, your team, your organization, or anyone you know. Feel free to text or call me at (850) 619-3576, shoot me an email at my personal email justinmears26@gmail.com or my LeadOff email justin@leadoffllc.com, or reach out on social media:

Twitter: @jmears26, @leadoffllc
Facebook: jmears26, leadoffllc
Instagram: @jmears26, @leadoffllc
LinkedIn: https://www.linkedin.com/in/justinmears26/